JOANNA GEYER-KORDESCH has had a distinguished academic career bridging the disciplines of history of medicine and cultural history as embodied in our landscapes. After becoming the first woman to direct The Wellcome Unit for the History of Medicine at the University from 1990 to 2001, she became Professor of European Natural History and History of Medicine at that university where, after retiring in 2006, she remains a Professor Emerita. Since retirement Joanna has continued her research interests while developing a parallel career as a poet, artist and creative essayist. In this latest phase of her life, following a debilitating illness, gardens have become central to her thinking, as well as places of healing, stimulus and reflection.

DONALD SMITH is a storyteller, novelist, playwright and founding Director of the Scottish Storytelling Centre. Donald's non-fiction books include *Freedom and Faith* on the Independence debate, *Pilgrim Guide to Scotland* which recovers the nation's sacred geography and four books, co-authored with Stuart McHardy, in the Luath Press Journeys and Evocations series. Donald has also written a series of historical novels, most recently *Flora McIvor*. He is currently Director of the Scottish International Storytelling Festival.

Why Gardens Matter

JOANNA GEYER-KORDESCH

with

Donald Smith

Luath Press Limited

EDINBURGH

www.luath.co.uk

First published 2020

ISBN: 978-1-912147-94-6

The paper used in this book is recyclable. It is made from low chlorine
pulps produced in a low energy, low emission manner
from renewable forests.

Printed and bound by CPI Antony Rowe, Chippenham

Typeset in 11 point Sabon by Carrie Hutchison

Contents

Acknowledgements

THE SEED OF *Why Gardens Matter* was nurtured by a series of talks and discussions presented at the Royal Botanic Garden in Edinburgh as part of the 2015 Scottish International Storytelling Festival. It was then developed following my debilitating stroke. It is illustrated by historical prints and sketches and poems from the journals I kept during my long period of recuperation.

My love of conversations brought this book to life. In the first days of my stroke I realised that I could not say words of any kind out loud – I then knew how crucial communication was. I visualised words. And this was when I received comfort, encouragement, kindness and sympathy. Those near me did not treat me as un-knowledgeable, unlearned or disabled in my mind.

Thank you all heartily. But especially Jim Paterson, my husband; Donald Smith, Director of the Scottish International Storytelling Festival at the Storytelling Centre; Gavin MacDougall at Luath Press who accepted my book for publication; Alice Young and Carrie Hutchison (Luath Press), who did so much in assisting me in bringing the book to fruition both in words and artwork; and Lauren Grieve (Luath Press), who realised how difficult it is for people with disabilities to get out and about and hold talks. I also want to thank everyone who worked on this book for their patience and words of encouragement, and those special people everywhere that take the time and trouble to help those with disabilities.

Introduction

GARDENS HAVE A special place for each and every one of us. Whether owning one, planting one, or just looking at different gardens while ambling down the street, they are part of our lives. They matter. And in many more ways than we might imagine.

This book puts gardens and their history at its core, but in a different way. The many and varied historical gardens make a claim on our attention. It is interesting to know what meanings were attached to them. But, beyond these actual gardens, there is also the garden of our mind and imagination. This garden too is very real. It allows us to perceive gardens as stories, as projections and as part of our emotions and feelings. We do not just try to keep a garden next to the house or go for a walk in the park; we can let plants speak to us as we become part of their growth. This is encountering gardens as places of healing. Both aspects are vital.

In the garden you can plant up, dig and mulch, wait for roots to take hold, watch for flowers to emerge and dead-head the roses to let them bloom afresh. There is always plenty to do. In fact, there is no end to the garden chores. In spring all the plants come out and start showing in a new green. The anticipation is high. The buds swell. The leaves show in their sweetest and lightest and most innocent, fresh, childlike colours.

It is this seasonal change which is important. It seems conventional and not worth noticing except for the labour it demands – the weeding and the pruning. But change also carries the message that we alter and we age. To do this gracefully, we can think of how the garden expresses time's passing.

After spring, summer comes. And there is a riot. Every bush and tree and flowerbed pushes out its own colourful glory. The variety of hues and shapes is endless. Roses abound, in small patio dimensions or tall tea-roses, or perhaps climbers and ramblers. Diversity abounds; daisies in many shapes have mostly a white beauty, but there are also Leucanthemums with a faint yellow. Kniphofias are red-hot pokers. Lavateras, or mallows, run wild. Petunias fill baskets or pots, and they too are multi-coloured. These random names call up only a few flowers which ring their changes all summer long. The season rolls on with cone flowers, a prairie plant in white or red or yellow. Monardas are now acclimatised in Scotland to brighten the late summer scene.

Then there is autumn with its decline, but also its striking features. The trees dominate with their change in colour. They begin to mutate their green into more riotous tones. Scarlet, yellow and brown fill out the hazy sunshine that is the best of the season's bowing out. Autumn means letting go. The leaves fall. The shrubs join the chorus. Even some small plants turn a startling red before they let their leaves drift loose. The winds get up. Bareness begins to dominate. The branches show their hitherto secret structures. Then pale trunks become mighty. The vibrant shades of green are gone.

Winter has set in. Now there is time for meditation. Now the bare earth becomes visible. The rivers flow past vegetation turned brown. There is a possibility of snow. Everyone shivers in the falling temperature. Our planet rotates away from the sun.

This book will follow this cycle to learn from high and low points, from the flowers, shrubs and trees changing in each season, as well as from the different ways gardens have followed the seasons. It is not a manual on how-to-garden; instead it expresses why gardens matter in human terms. Whether real or in the mind, gardens refresh the spirit. This book seeks to encourage everyone to stop and listen to how things grow and fade and grow and fade again. Gardens can do this for real and in the imagination. The reader should do both. Instead of fighting to have city lights, radiators turned on and hiding in the house the reader can glory in nature. Especially in winter when nature seems to go underground, reflection is penetrating, silent and worthwhile.

There should be space for deliberation in cold winter. Few things are flourishing above ground, yet roots are developing, where we cannot see them. Like thoughts they need the time and space of bareness to reach glorious colour. The silence nurtures strength. The pauses are natural and beneficial.

Why Gardens Matter is for those who garden for real and those who cannot. The encounter with a fictional garden is also of value. The idea of this book is that no one should be left out – least of all children, the elderly or those with disabilities. One of the great virtues of gardening is the ability of plants to come up green out of a rough brown or black soil and even to bloom when neglected. Gardens can be enjoyed in books. It was, for example, crucial in the 1860s when children began to be the subjects of stories on their own account, that gardens became their creative places. Children were read to and adults encouraged the little ones to bring gardens and nature into their homes.

Imaginary gardens are appreciated by all ages. They provide more than herbal cures: they are the deep well of healing. Some can be visited in the imagination and in reality. The hermitages, groves, temples, cascades and waterfalls constructed in 18th century landscape gardens reflect thoughts and emotions. They are the constructions of people with their ability to make you linger and meditate, to imagine and remember.

Lingering and meditating, what the Picturesque and the Romantics called 'the insights of solitude', were essential to landscape gardens. But this is not time-bound. Today the natural landscapes of the famous 'Capability' Brown, who assembled clumps of trees, lakes and lawns around patrician houses, makes one aware of natural space and the capacity to dream too. Each person striding and stopping in these wide, nature-imitating spaces learns to take themselves seriously. The landscape is designed to give vistas into a rural infinity. To arrest cares and woes, or to think more deeply upon them, or to dispel them, is the essence of all landscape gardens.

This mirrors, curiously enough, the search for paradise or the paradise of the imagination in children's literature. The healing garden is just that: healing means not standing still, in the mind or physically. Through meditation on plants or views, or garden art, a movement of thought is engendered, alongside physical journeys. It was the children in *The Secret Garden* who became aware of the silent language of growth. They became different from the stunted selves each had thought epitomised them. They were born into tyrannising others and they learned through the growth in gardens that they could be better than that. Nature, although not speaking in a direct voice, gave them space and inspiration enough to seek fresh air and be healed – to find happiness.

'The child is father of the man', so the saying goes, and all genders are included. There is truth in that, especially when contemplating change. This life is certainly not static. Healing gardens point in the right direction. Whether accepting the thorns on the rose or the beauty of the petals, all is change and growth. Rainer Maria Rilke, the poet, famously said that under so many rose petals there is a contemplation of emptiness. We should knowingly accept and absorb this 'emptiness' to induce healing.

Such is the intention. This is a book to find locations and to develop ourselves. It is not here to command or provide solutions; its reason for existence is openness – to find, to imagine and to grow.

🙵 🙵 🙵

Gardens are all around us. This book will give you an overview of their history. Armed with this knowledge you can go and enjoy them more fully. The history allows insight, but our presence in the garden, in all its aspects, is your own. Being able to learn about gardens leads us to love them, their stories and just what it is that speaks to us, Then they give us the joy of being there in every weather, each mood of the season. In the second part of *Why Gardens Matter* we explore these creative responses.

Myriad garden books talk about the planting. This is important if you are creating a garden, but standing in one is just as important. Landscape gardens are about meditation more than planning where to situate trees, lakes and shrubs. Looking along a sightline and locating a ruin – usually an artificial one placed strategically in order to contemplate the passing of time – is equally significant. Many gardens of the past are arranged to bring the visitor up short or to have them puzzle over which direction to take. This is well thought out since stopping and thinking creates worthwhile crossroads before embarking on the one road or the other.

In the history of gardens there are of course distinctive variations. Some gardens are good for looking and taking a meandering path. Some gardens are made to be enclosed. Some gardens are scented and give you back what is lost in memory. Some provide green space for a much-needed pause. To engage with specifics you can read the appropriate book or gather the best advice. But whatever or wherever you are in this designed space of 'second' nature, the thread of the healing garden will entwine with aspects of the human spirit. The bare soil and luxurious flowers are partners. You need an elemental root below to throw a flower up. Good soil is needed for growth. Who knows what may flourish then – what grows is not only the flower which you see.

❧

PART ONE
HISTORIC GARDENS

The Medieval and Monastery Garden

THE HEALING GARDEN is not there for just the physical. It encompasses the mind and emotions. It can and should help us cope with the ups and downs experienced in life and always make us remember joy as well as pain.

Folk cures looked not just to the healing power of herbs, but to the chants and invocations which accompanied them. These invoked the great chain of being where everything was spiritual as well as physical. God as well as mud or worms had a settled hierarchy. The unseen powers of the healers in Celtic cultures often evoked the human by crying to divine power to grant mastery over pain and suffering. The healers were the trained and knowledgeable advocates of the Divine who acted together with the sufferer.

These chants and prayers went into realms we consider strange today. We do not often see the need to delve deep into uncanny powers. But Scottish Gaelic folklore did; and these customs persisted for centuries and are still practised today. What remains meaningful is the invocation of something more than the individual ailment: the inclusion of that single element in all the powers that be. It is not the isolation of illness or pain, but what it has in common with dynamic forces we cannot see. If you believe that what happens is fortuitous, there may be a greater whole included in the workings of both mind and body.

The medieval garden inherits that philosophy but also goes in the direction of sensory pleasure. Abbeys and priories, which welcomed the sick and gave succour to the traveller, gloried in the paradise that was the church, heaven on earth. They allowed walks in their orchards of blossom to revive the soul, while tread-

ing the same orchards with baskets full of autumnal fruit for the
table. Planted with healing herbs, their gardens allowed for a
cure beyond this physical medicine, an inestimable, allusive and
powerful scent that transcended the earthly wear and tear. Introducing calmness where there seemed to be turmoil, the cloister
attached to the church was a place to think more extensively and
quietly. It was a place to slow down. This is as true today as of
the past.

In contrast to later gardens, the medieval garden was small
and conducive either to romance or retreat. Medieval gardens
had seats in bowers, and in the square and oblong lawns, and
well-cultivated plants with symbolic meanings on show. These
gardens in time intermingled with old manuscript paintings in
Herbals and devotional primers. The sweet scented white lily is
not only exemplary to grow, but speaks of purity and headiness
in ethereal ways. Heaven is thus connected with earth. Roses too,
the old-fashioned ones grown in the medieval gardens such as the
rosa alba, the rosa gallica, the dog rose and the damask rose had
meanings beyond their use. They bloomed only once, at the end
of May and in June, so conveying allusions to moral perfections
and the passing of beauty.

There are many possible places to start examining the importance of the garden through time. But, in terms of the garden and
its significance to humankind, a good place to begin is with their
medieval development, both as a place to grow plants for food
and for medicine and also as a place for enjoyment and exercise of
the mind. It seems that we must continually rediscover the truth
of these core purposes. The first Herbals in manuscript form described plants and flowers alongside their medicinal uses. They
were familiar to the Greeks, translated by the Arabs and applied
by learned medieval monks. Treatment of the ill meant a study
of plants and their characteristics, and this grew into a fine art
dependent on scrutinising leaves, stems, flowers and roots. It was
anything but a simple operation: those who could see what was

Engraved title page of John Gerard's Herball, *with representations of Theophrastus and Dioscorides, 1636. (Wellcome Collection. Attribution 4.0 International (CC BY 4.0))*

effective, when and how to apply it, were highly valued and this knowledge built on the tradition of Herbals.

Dioscorides, in his famous *De Materia Medica*, developed the Herbal in manuscript form that everyone referred to and used for centuries beyond its inception, around 500 AD. Later Herbals also included plants from further north with descriptions of new plants that were encountered in specific regions. It was practical to have plants specified in the medical sense, but also described for their own sake. Alas, the Herbals and their illustrations did not distinguish old from new. The theoretical knowledge of plants was there, but usage was increasingly dependent on being familiar with what actually grew in the ground.

By medieval times, salvation of the physical body, as well as of the soul, was in the hands of learned monks and abbots, who advanced their knowledge in special gardens near their infirmaries. Monks increasingly lived many tiered working lives, centred on communal prayer and private silence, but practising advanced study, horticulture, open hospitality and care for the ill. Those who could read did so in several languages, especially Latin. Herbals were often in this tongue as well as later in the vernacular. They had plant descriptions in words and pictures, but these were often stylised. You had to know the herbs in practice alongside the description in the book or manuscript, as there was always the danger of applying the wrong plant or the wrong dosage.

As the manuscripts were converted to printed books, after 1470, plants were valued more and more for their specific characteristics in their locality and were recorded in this way for publication. The plants whose features were delineated became objects whose natural qualities were worthy of study in their own right. In a sense the written and printed Herbals were the first books to demand that plants be characterised apart from their medicinal use. In this way medicine helped evolve the description and classification of plants into taxonomy and botany.

The monks in their cloisters were not dispensers of health as we understand it. They knew the efficacy of herbs, but they considered health to be both physical and spiritual. Even today the lore of herbs is not just physical. Enticing smells were as important as the division of plants into their organic parts. The cloisters were places of walking and meditating. The garden as an experience was as important as the medicinal properties of the plants that grew there. Pleasing odour was what sent those deep in thought heavenwards, not earthwards. Many flowers included in these cloisters were sweet smelling, and symbolically conveyed that the Virgin Mary or saints were present. There was not a great divide between these invisible presences and belief. Flowers and herbs were prevalent in enclosed gardens near the church and often accessible only through the church.

When the cloister garth, as it was called, remained green and grassy, it was meant for relaxation, a refreshment of the eyes, but nonetheless it was a constant reminder of the goodness of God. Flowers had their own language and this reached down to Victorian times, when composed bouquets were devised and presented. These meanings have however evolved. During the dominance of the Roman Catholic Church, before the Reformation, most roses and lilies referred to Mary, the mother of Jesus. Other faiths had their symbolic flowers too, extending the meaning of each flower to the spiritual realm. The mix of floral scent and meaning was part of spiritual life – herbs too had scent and meaning, but it was more applied. The expression through flowers, their colour, scent and even just their presence, can still elevate us into the spiritual realm. The symbolic meaning of flowers combines with their natural beauty to help each person to go beyond just the floral composition. The spiritual realm opens avenues of exploration of many kinds from joyousness to steady calm.

Most abbots were versed in medicine. St Benedict had delineated two essential rules: one was to accept all travellers; the other was to heal the sick. Although not all orders were of

Two medieval lovers in a garden at Château de Chantilly, France.
(© Thaliastock / Mary Evans)

Benedictine descent most communities followed these rules. The great religious orders were international communities. This led to extensive grounds and innumerable networks across the world as the more powerful among them travelled. Monasteries were lively places, dedicated to God, but also busy fulfilling the necessities of life. The monks tended to grow crops as well as the smaller gardens of herbs and flowers. They had orchards in their care; the fruit trees included pears, cherries, plums, quinces, almonds, mulberries and varieties of apples. Orchards were not only there for food. In the spring they provided colour and sweetness. New trees and new seeds were received from many sources, drawing on the international connections between the orders.

Self-sufficiency was important to each community. There were fish ponds for meals, the orchards for fruit in different seasons and herbs for flavour. Plots were in rows within designated areas. The rows could be readily managed from each side. This regimen of types of herbs, types of flowers and edible plants allowed for rotation. Some were left to lie fallow, a practice common in most gardens, but inspired here by the Biblical belief in a 'Sabbath' rest.

As the social scale moved upwards and outside monasteries, the garden became courtly and treasured as an elite preserve. In these activities beyond the monasteries, behaviour became more secular. Gardens invited dances, music and romance. This courtly behaviour went with castles and knights and ladies. It is how we idealise these long-ago times. Some of these gardens still survive in their sadly scant records and beautiful illustrations. On the castellated towers the wide view went out over forested lands enclosing wild beasts. These lands were walled in and the pheasants, rabbits, hares, deer and sometimes exotics, were held in these pleasant enclosures until hunted. Smaller enclosures were made within the walled garden, mostly using trellises of flowers and vines. Seats were placed in these small formal gardens, or herbers, upon which ladies and gentlemen sat, alone or conversing.

There were many variants, but all the herbers were tight enclosures and sweet smelling, whether from white or red old roses,
lilies or violets. Many of the basic plants we have today have
their origins in the medieval centuries. They were specially planted and cultivated in the geometric layouts of lawns and flowers
in the herbers. Walls and trellises kept them safely enclosed and
bowers and small trees provided shade, while water or fountains
made soothing sounds. The Virgin Mary is often depicted in such
gardens holding the infant Jesus.

Pathways lead around the herber and within orchards and
pleasure gardens. None of the careful lawns, sweet smelling beds,
orchards in bloom or with fruit were without walks. Reading,
meditating or conversing were the preferred activities in these verdant gardens. It is as if the thoughts expressed in medieval gardens
reach out, heightening awareness of an ordered life where each
person has many tasks to fulfil, while traversing through many
patterns of growth and so many different experiences of life.

Pathways and seats in the herber were for thinking and reflecting. The whole meditative life of medieval times was an in-
tertwining of hard and short lived years with an order that went
far beyond the merely physical. The spiritual life, or that of sin-
cere emotion, ran toward completion in individual realisation. It
grasped immateriality as an essence. Life was, so to speak, too
short to delve into the merely material.

When the monarchs of Scotland founded their abbeys and
priories, they not only saw heaven on earth reaching up in stone
pillars and prayer ascending with their spiritual needs. They were
investing in a whole array of community support, from hours in
divine supplication for the living and the dead, through to tending the sick and infirm. Later centuries would arrange gardens to
set off the remains of abbeys and priories in their ruined state,
half covered in green shoots of ivy, but this was a sad retrospect
wrought by the Reformation. In their heyday monasteries were
efficacious centres of healing and sanctuary.

Two royal figures sit in their enclosed garden in medieval Britain from In Feudal Times *by EM Tappan. (Mary Evans Picture Library/TAH Collection)*

A traveller in time might be surprised when discovering that medieval Scotland was endowed with so many monastic gardens. They are now almost all gone, only imaginable where they might have been among ruins. Nonetheless, they can be recreated as fertile ground among the spectacular remains that were once abbeys or priories. One of Iona's glories is its gardens, not least the re-imagined nuns' cloister with its sunk lawns and herbaceous borders. In an image of St Andrew's Cathedral's cloisters, the symbolic tree of life grows. This tree has significance in the rectangle where the monks prayed. It reveals where they rooted their theology, while also dispensing their herbal medicine. As we have seen, they both grew and administered those remedies. Their pruning and harvesting showed respect for countless trees,

The ruins of Dryburgh Abbey near Edinburgh. (Mary Evans Picture Library)

vegetables and flowers. Their skills were known in terms of good land usage as much as spiritual counsel.

The monks and lay brothers belonged to orders deeply anchored in the then universal medieval Catholic Church. The Benedictines, the Cistercians, the Dominicans, the Augustinians, the Carthusians, to name some of them, built not only churches, but a whole complex of houses and lands under cultivation, as their dominion. Most were dissolved in the Reformation of the 1560s. It was a time of great turmoil, and the abbeys and priories were surrounded by graveyards. Where there had been much tending of the land, interspersed with an obligation to prayer, there were now copious ruins.

But, even in the 18th century, memories remained of the medieval garden. Good pears from ancient trees, some thought to be more than 200 years old, were still to be found in the 1700s. Although the land, and those who owed allegiance to the monasteries, had been secularised and transferred in ownership (many to the lords of the manor), productive orchards and vegetable patches still gave of their best.

These survivals should feed into the imagination. Faced with crumbling walls and arches, now bare and open to the sky, we travel back. Ancient trees and traditional plants evoke a world of feeling. What I remember most from visits to such sites are the swallows and swifts flying under and over these bare, ruined choirs. At Rievaulx Abbey in the North York Moors, the stonework is open to the blue sky; the ruins became part of a landscape garden. Visitors were meant to contemplate these ruins. I thought of many people I venerated, including those of centuries past, and watched the black-winged birds darting in and out, with nests high in the vaulting. It was spring. Rievaulx Abbey was the mother to all Cistercian foundations in England and Scotland before it became integrated into the Duncombe landscape garden.

Near Edinburgh there are numerous monastic ruins. Among the imposing ones are those in the Borders, not far from each other. Dryburgh Abbey is now surrounded by exotic trees at their full height, planted at some remove. It adds to the ruins to have them surrounded by tall and imposing specimens. They frame the light-coloured stones of the vaulting church and its cloisters. Not much remains but the masonry and indications of altars at which masses were once said are still eloquent. It must have been lively, with the comings and goings of congregations and busy monks.

The gardens are no longer extant. But the church, tall and settled in its grass, has acquired new meditative possibilities. From the firs, the cedars and deciduous trees, thoughts wander to the centuries of stone and the spiritual values that went with them. It raises feelings of exchange between living beauty and long ago. Dryburgh Abbey and its ruins is where Sir Walter Scott chose to be buried.

The living and the dead are invariably mixed in these con-
templations. It behoves us to remember this when studying the
mighty abbeys of the Borders. They were given over to powerful lay landowners. Yet their ruins remain to remind us of
both the Reformation's critique of the Catholic faith and that
through historic turmoil nothing on Earth is permanent. Even
the herbal remedies of the monks and their arduous working
of the monastic lands resulted in impermanence. Yet their legacy endures.

The medicinal gardens and orchards are lost. But to recollect
in sweetness and light, to contemplate troubles and to wander
in peace among weathered arches is just the same as in the past.
In the fine volume, *Scotland's Lost Gardens*, Albertus Magnus
is quoted describing the cloister. He says there should be lawns
and places to sit and meditate. Behind these should be well-scent-
ed flowers, such as violets, lilies and roses. And there should be
herbs that cure and add their scent too. In this peaceful enclave
people will relax and think more of eternal things.

Albert the Great was pointing out the beneficial uses attached
to abbeys, cathedrals and priories. Although the gardens were
lost or secularised in Scotland, their regenerative power and their
central role continued in the Catholic countries of the Coun-
ter-Reformation. And Scotland did not cut itself off from Europe.
Abbots, bishops and the nobility knew and learned from being
abroad and their contacts there. Some church leaders still had to
go to Rome and the nobility often married aristocrats from the
Netherlands, Spain, France, Italy or Austria. Students went to
universities across Europe and trade expanded.

In Klosterneuburg, Austria, the same legend as that of David I of Scotland exists about a stag with a holy cross between
the antlers that led to the foundation of an abbey. David I too,
as he encountered the stag, in peril for his life, saw a vision and
founded Holyrood Abbey. The Austrian Monarch of medieval
times did the same in Klosterneuburg. The spiritual origins of

great complexes as large as these can be the same though almost a continent apart.

Along the Danube River there are many places that are monasteries still, some hidden in valleys, such as the Cistercian Zwettl Abbey, in a remote valley towards the border with Slovakia north of the Danube. Or they are widely seen on the mountain tops, such as at Goettweig, or the Augustinian Melk Abbey or Altenburg Abbey on a rise in Lower Austria. In an old painting of Altenburg an orchard is shown, which is surely much like the orchards cultivated by the religious orders and their labourers in the great Scottish abbeys.

These grand monasteries in Austria are predominantly of Baroque splendour dedicated to the Virgin Mary. They are still inhabited by monks and their devout practices. And they still have gardens and orchards. Many of these are there now for the monks to walk and meditate and are largely private, but there are also gardens open to the public. Many are quiet places and ideal for solitude and silence. The gardens and cloisters were places for reading, writing and meditation. The first two were considered an art in times when few could practise such skills. Meditation is still valued, but places for such solitude and introversion are becoming scarce. Lost gardens are like the lost monasteries of Scotland. But herbal gardens became part of medicinal practice beyond the holy precincts. In Edinburgh, the Royal Botanic Garden is worth visiting to see how herbal medicine has changed. It has its origins not in monks' knowledge, but in the interests of the well-travelled community of Scottish doctors. Like members of the clergy, the nobility, merchants and scholars they continued travelling in Europe and building on medieval connections.

The whole world was gradually being explored and gardens in far places were eagerly sought out because new and unknown plants interested professionals as well as committed lay people. Existing gardens were planted with exotic plants as well as those with medicinal uses. Doctors had an abiding interest in herbal and vegetative cures, including those nurtured and cultivated by monks centuries before. In the monastery garden, as well as the secular garden, there is a reconciliation between the sacred and the earthly. This union of spiritual and practical things remains in our gardens today, as our unfolding story will reveal.

Parterres

THE PARTERRE GARDEN, fashionable in the 16th and 17th centuries, was imported first from Italy. The land that loved water on its more arid planes with canals, grottoes and lakes ruled over by the gods of rivers and oceans. These original parterres were haphazard in form, but the great nation of the Sun King, Louis XIV, tamed them to the scope of imperial France. André Le Nôtre reshaped the countryside and made it into the parks that suited royal grandeur. Le Nôtre was one of the newly fashionable, and greatest, of the French garden designers. The Sun King recruited him to plan Versailles, while the exiled King Charles II also learned from Le Nôtre and subsequently brought Le Nôtre's conception of gardens to Britain when he was restored to his throne in 1660.

Parterre gardens are elaborately designed, with formal embellishments which were usually looked down upon from castles or grand houses. They were reasoned, logical, symmetrical and regular, but with enough variety to bolster the soul. The noble visitor gazed along a central axis, meant to end in the far countryside. The eye was lured to the rim of the world, represented by mysterious woods. Not only were you lord of the manor, but lord of all.

Parterres are like stitch work: curvaceous, inventive, elaborate, containing plants in geometric arrangements, with pebbles, earthwork or gravel in between. Every parterre is an appropriate event, made in honour of the owners, taking away any boredom from looking out the window by reminding them of grandeur and extraordinary deeds. In these flat, abstract patterns there are desires and statements that may not mean the same to us in the present time. They are as abstract and sometimes mysterious as emblems or coats of arms.

Some of these intentions are rolled out within hedges, usually box and yew, which were cut to order, opening the space around the vertical house in horizontal rectangular shapes. More elaborately, you would often find more box hedges and an inner core of fanciful patterns reaching out from either side of the garden. In the farther distance there might be a grotto, or a fountain with nymphs or a canal. All these features were along an axis, while extending enough to make you wander in either direction from the main path.

These gardens engaged the eye above all. They were dominated by their castles and bordered by the real wilderness around them. Their tight, even-bodied squares enclosed with green hedging made a feast for the mind, set against the wild irregularity of nature. They became sophisticated artforms, schooled against nature, seeing it as untamed, a force the incursion of which would engulf man. That is why parterre designs seem to be striding out to dominate their environment. Nature was conquered so that it could be bent to human will, re-fashioned and displayed in homage.

In time the parterre fashion came to Scotland as well. One outstanding example remains at Drummond Castle, although it was subsequently reworked, and perhaps restored in different ways. The central parterre is now a thistle on a St Andrew's Cross. Trees grown to their maturity, plantings of Victorian or the early 20th century, obscure the terraces, but stand out gloriously in their seasons. Whether we catch all the original emblems and erudite pictorial references is now immaterial. What matters is gazing at this monument to nobility and the passage of more than 500 years. In essence, Drummond Castle and its garden hark back to medieval origins and their central design draws on the same principles.

The parterres at the foot of such a castle are easy to walk, yet inside the box hedging the routes are intricate, curvilinear, often planted in fanciful patterns. They puzzle and impress.

The garden at Drummond Castle, the design around a central saltire. (Mary Evans/Reginald A Malby & Co. Collection)

What they do is add to the dominance of the castle. It reaches out to these reflections of its medieval character. The white statues and topiary are like emblems that reveal and hide the messages, mute but learned in the garden. The statues can be of gods, or the elements or historical events, and the deep green of the yews or firs enhance them. Alternatively, the topiary can be cut into heraldic symbols, representing a reigning monarch or imperial order. In this way the formal garden takes on a political shape in accord with the allegiances of the owner.

The castle at Drummond retained its parterres because its family fought for a distinctively Scottish king, of the Stuart line, in the Jacobite Rising of 1745. The estate was forfeited to the crown and languished. In the 19th century it was decided by new owners to keep the gardens in parterres; but they were restored

Drumlanrig Castle grounds in 1879, the parterre can be seen in the foreground. (Mary Evans Picture Library)

or reinvented with the thistle and the saltire. Bonnie Prince Charlie was not however restored.

In the autumn, when the last leaves are turning, and the sun is low, striking shades of a fiery red light are cast on this towered mansion and its history. As you look, the mind reflects on past times and you recall the vicissitudes of such fortified habitations, the fears and joys of those who occupied them and the relevance of these emotions to the present day.

Drumlanrig Castle in Dumfries is another Scottish example of an old site which was then extensively constructed with the house as the main focus, but with terraces and parterres descending the slopes that had originally lent the place its natural strength. These gardens have now been renewed, and remain elaborate, though fewer in number than in the original concept.

Drumlanrig nestles in the hills and, when you are near, the parterres enhance the high towered, red sandstone building. Then, as you wander the flat and ornate parterres, some with their evergreen topiary, the gardens widen out. An infinite line is drawn which may end in the hills, or it may lose itself in the parkland which seem to stretch ever farther. The old trees of the parkland augment the formality of colours contained in the box hedging. This contrasting variety makes both aspects more vivid: the man-made patterns of the enclosures in squares are set in colourful opposition to the later-planted, now huge, specimen trees. At Drummond the castle ends in wide, sweeping parkland leading, in Scottish style, to the wider surrounding hills.

Parterres, the main sign of medieval gardens, do not however have to belong to any particular period or country. As described, they were imported from Italy first, then developed in grandeur by the Frenchman André Le Nôtre at Vicomte Le Vaux and the Sun King's Versailles. The gardens we have now in Britain are conglomerates of the French parterres and English landscape gardens, though the results are often happily merged. Time has wrought its own compositions around the original design.

The topiary of the parterre in its sombre evergreen is a reminder of events in medieval centuries, such as the crusades, with their voyages, captures, ransoms and adventures. In winter, when statues are hidden by protective wooden boxes, the topiary stands, often in snow, as a silent indicator of the years long since when the castle was built. A parterre has seen many things, then and now, and it may seem good to meditate on chance and frailty, the happenstance of life.

Avenues of trees, most often limes, lead to castles and houses at the centre of the site. These avenues are like arteries straight to the heart of the land. In every case, they begin a journey of revelation and mystery. Clothed in spring leaves or shed in the bright colours of their falling, they separate the outer world from the house and gardens. It is almost a secret place. The avenue

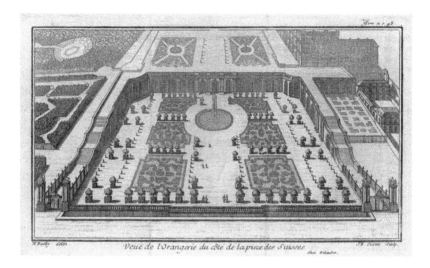

The Orangery at Versailles. (Mary Evans Picture Library)

functions as a separation from, and an introduction to, what will be discovered in the wider setting. The lore of the place becomes clear as a romantic discovery, faintly reflected in the brochures provided. Thinking and feeling the past is part of the experience and essential to why such gardens continue to matter.

The castles were built mainly on promontories in the land-scape, commanding a far view. Close to their windows were ter-races and where the ground flattened, but still with an overview, were the parterres, their statues, topiary and water features. It all came to a whole, demonstrating the slide from medieval times into the Renaissance. In these gardens the nobility held masques and commissioned music among many elite entertainments. These stately and intriguing feasts were held in what is now ghostly splendour; we can imagine them but not recreate them. Once I myself witnessed theatre of a grand scale in one of these gardens. It left a lasting impression: being 'out of this world' as I was suddenly caught in another time.

The inspiration for the gardens came from a nobility mindful of its power and relation to monarchs. Monarchs came to visit, such as Mary Queen of Scots in the 16th century at Craigmillar Castle, not far from Edinburgh. This was the stronghold of her loyal supporters, the Prestons. She was happy to take the air outside and to enjoy the atmosphere of a Loire château while remaining close to her capital city. She too looked down from the castle onto the parterres and was able to wander through the south facing precincts and to hold court in the gardens.

In Edinburgh itself there was a separate section of the old town called the Canongate, leading to the Abbey and then Palace of Holyroodhouse. This area was inhabited by nobles and merchants, each with their walled gardens. These had been developed from the original long plots of land that each inhabitant of the burgh owned with their house. Within them were the same parterres. They were fewer in number, but as intricate and geometric as those which proliferated below the windows and towers of the castles.

All of these formal gardens were of course were outshone by the extensive grounds that Mary and her garden loving mother,

The gardens of the Palais d'Orleans. (Wellcome Collection. Attribution 4.0 International (CC BY 4.0))

Marie de Guise, created at Holyroodhouse. They became a strong
bond between the long-separated mother and daughter. There is
some originating sense here of the love of gardens that was to
characterise Scots of all classes through to the present.

Everyone could walk in such gardens and enjoy the layouts,
with their combination of overall order with an intimacy and deft-
ness of detail. Here was something to show and admire, something
to wander amongst and glory in, as the human hand had enabled
artifice to cap nature. On the other hand, the formality confined
and divided. Such gardens reinforced hierarchy with its separation
of the classes. Yet something that integrated all the gardens was
the need for food. The fruit trees that graced all kinds of gardens
attest to this need. So do the fish ponds, the kailyards and the
dovecotes on the grounds of the wealthier estates. Each served its
purpose in the elaborate feasts brought to table and in basic daily
sustenance. Gardens were not just places in which to take the air
marvelling at their artistry, but practical enterprises devoted to
serving up the foodstuffs and delicacies of the season.

Gardens were walled enclosures places protected against forag-
ing animals, wild and domestic, as well as human poachers. Later
these walls also contained kitchen gardens, from where vegetables,
fruits and herbs were harvested. But long before the great change in
the 18th and 19th century to landscape gardens, the vista already
reigned. Fruit trees and ornamental geometry, enclosures and the
wild, could be seen in an instant. It seemed, and was meant to seem,
that beyond the castle the estate lands stretched on and on. Families
of note around the world gazed beyond the terraces and pretty parterres of their ancestral holdings, displaying their wealth and power.

Yet this ideal of gardens was to outlive the worldly pomp of
their owners and was to contribute to how all classes and nations
were to value gardens for centuries to come. We are still heirs of the
parterre.

Landscape Gardens

JUST AS THE monastic gardens fed into wider medieval gardens, and then the formal parterres of the 16th and 17th centuries, so many previous features were absorbed into the 18th century, contributing to the new fashion for landscape gardens. In fact, even as Enlightenment thinkers and designers invented 'the modern', they consciously harked back to the classical world and to the villas and landscapes of Italy.

Their journey back through time illuminated the joys of seeing a garden, or of walking in gardens that evoked a past age. They were meant to create islands of thought, lifted out of time. For example, the Latin poet Virgil's writing on landscapes was held to define 'the bucolic' or pastoral. This was what relaxing in nature was all about. The contemplation of a waterfall, like the one built by William Shenstone at The Leasowes, offered the sound of cascading water alongside the feeling that one could reflect alone with pleasure in the enjoyment of such a countryside. The fast-moving, downwards spiralling cascade was in honour of the Roman Virgil. It dominates the scene of the circuitous walk and it is meant to concentrate the mind. In the end, it matters that the gushing, rushing water flows forth in the grove of trees, while the walk on which its running course is appreciated has its own complementary direction or dynamic.

One scion of the great architectural dynasty of Scotland, John Adam, incorporated ideas from this southern landscape garden at his home in Merchiston, north of Edinburgh. His aim was to blend the reading of the classics, so important then, with sociability including enjoyable family gatherings. Both home and learning were dear to his heart. The landscape garden expressed both possibilities. Everyone was potentially included in enjoying

North Merchiston House, John Adam's home, drawn from nature
by Alexander Archer, 1837. (© Courtesy of HES (Alexander
Archer Collection) Canmore)

them both and all it took was a walk, together or alone, to call up
the experience. Gardens had come to matter in new ways. Portrait painters took to portraying their subjects along with friends
and family in a domestic landscape outside.

In the 18th century Scottish Enlightenment, when European
ideals were thought out and debated in this northern country,
landscape gardens were one of the few places where the Picturesque and the Romantic stood firm against reason alone. There
is something refreshing in nature being its own moody self, a not
always predictable playmate. Scottish gardens followed many
traits of English ones, which featured first around the River
Thames. However, landscape gardens in Scotland were planned
in variation to English ones; they were designed differently

The Leasowes in 1788, the residence of Edward Horne, the gardens were laid out by the poet William Shenstone. (Mary Evans Picture Library)

because the hills and lochs offered equally pleasing, yet wilder, countryside settings. In this way an intuitive strength resided in the much-altered gardens of the century of rationalism. Though products of the Enlightenment, these gardens pay tribute to a landscape they did not conceive. The hills and lochs were not man-made. Nature held her place alongside Reason.

The sightlines designed for these gardens looked out to the contours created by nature, giving those who walked in them a double perspective. As people strolled past lawns, statues and ornaments, water features, houses and arranged trees, their gaze was directed outwards.

Notable in all the twists and turns of the paths is the invitation to venture beyond the immediate object. None of the circuitous walks of a landscape garden are just land, lochs and trees. Every single twist and turn steps beyond itself, and it is this surprising act of pointing every which way that makes the garden routes a wonder unto themselves. Horizons are widened and imagination engaged, as we embark on a journey that unfolds like the chapters of a story.

The more the visitor looks and sees, the more emotion and reason succumb and let go; we segue into a world that enlists all our faculties to make everything whole and new. We become like Adam and Eve in the Garden of Eden. Pictures are gleaned by looking outward, raising the head to the many features beyond. Also, like those primal humans, we have been gifted the ability to describe and recall what is seen. Such recollections are like reading a text which involves a more inward reflective turn. But this too is brought about by and depends on the first sensory and emotional stimulus – the upfront art of a garden designer, not to mention the labour of the working gardeners.

The landscape garden of the early 18th century prided itself in the contact made with the gods and goddesses, mainly Greek or Roman. In its statuary or its temples, it referred to mythological beings and was happy to re-imagine their stories. Such stories were multi-layered. Temples were the homes of gods like the owner had his residence, but the allusions were also part of the landscape. People gazed at and entered temples, but the temple pointed to meanings in the wider landscape.

For example, the valley at Stourhead has its Pantheon facing the visitor as soon as he or she begins the circuit of the lake. The Pantheon is a temple dedicated to all the gods and goddesses. It contains the statues of divinities that mattered to the designer of the garden, Henry Hoare, nicknamed 'The Magnificent'. Among these gods were Hercules and Meleander, two male demi-gods that were popular at the time. But also present were the goddesses Diana, Isis and Ceres or Flora. Hoare wanted his visitors to encounter the divine, but to consider more than just their divinity. Hercules and his many labours were suggested in order to remind viewers of this hero's strict allegiance to the narrow and rocky path of virtue rather than the easy-going highway of licentiousness. The goddesses too were there for contemplation and edification. Isis, for example, was the revered life-giving mother of nature and humankind.

The Pantheon as a whole is a reminder that beings other than humans reign in nature. We must align with these, benevolent or malign, if we are to be attentive beyond the tiny circle of experience that we consider when we focus solely on material things. The landscape garden mattered as an immediate experience but also as a fount of cultural values, even as the Industrial Revolution gathered pace to change tracts of Britain's countryside beyond recognition.

In 18th century Scottish landscape gardens too there were temples and they evoked these associations with the gods, while their views stretched further, inviting contemplation of the wilder landscape. In the design of Inveraray Castle, for example, undertaken by Archibald, 3rd Duke of Argyll, this added vista expanded the array of mountains, wooded hills, river and loch around the castle, in the characteristic Scottish setting. Moreover, the turrets and high-backed bridges over a sham moat were one of the first signs of the Gothic manner. Inveraray was also one of the first great houses to be erected like a castle, although never intended to be defensive like its real counterparts in medieval times. All these design features augmented the unique, but hard won, visibility of what is even now the main feature of a striking landscape at the head of Loch Fyne.

Castles designed to heighten the naturally dramatic Highland contours became favourites among the writers of the 18th and early 19th centuries; and later examples such as Eilean Donan Castle were to dominate tourist driven perspectives on the Highlands into modern times. Sir John Dalrymple was a notable early exponent on a par with renowned writers dedicated to

*The gardens at Stourhead, seen from the Mount of Diana around
1760. (Mary Evans Picture Library)*

landscape gardens. He highlighted scenic Scottish exemplars,
placed among hills and lochs. His book, written in early 1760
and circulated, among others, to the poet William Shenstone, and
was published much later in 1823 as *An Essay on Landscape
Gardening*.

The specifics of the Scottish landscape garden are perhaps
what nurtured a heightened Romantic awareness of a land riv-
en by inlets and girded by rocky shores. This is highlighted in
The Book of the Scottish Garden produced by the Royal Botanic
Gardens of Scotland. Torosay Castle is one of the first locations
mentioned as approached by sea:

> To explore the gardens of Scotland is to follow a fascinating
> trail full of surprises left by personalities of the past and con-
> stantly added to by new owners and gardeners. If you look
> very hard, you might catch a glimpse of the statues as the
> ferry approaches Torosay on the Isle of Mull.[1]

Far and near, there are eye-openers in every landscape garden, especially on their trails 'full of surprises'. Perhaps one of the best surprises is these ever-changing perspectives on the sea in the Scottish gardens. Ardmore House has a seascape as rich as Torosay Castle, which itself looks across the bay to Duart Castle and beyond it to McCaig's Tower, Oban. The temperate garden at Inverewe also features tantalising glimpses of the sea. Watery elements added to the mythological inhabitants of most landscape gardens, not least William Shenstone's The Leasowes.

Locations multiplied and influenced each other across Britain. John Adam was a pioneer at Edinburgh's North Merchiston House, though he was forced to sell the estate due to financial losses. His garden was a bucolic idyll re-defining what Scottish scenery meant. He was influenced by the intimate effects achieved by William Kent. Kent and his mentor, Lord Burlington, began the planned country house and garden at Chiswick sitting on the verge of London. This new creation by Burlington and Kent was based on a Palladian villa in the countryside. What distinguished these classical, originally Italian, villas was their setting out of towns in the agricultural fields.

Their outlook was striking, as was their elevation above the landscape with elegant columns and a capping tympanum framing the steps leading to their main portals. Sometimes on the roof there was another lookout over the fields, endowed with a further set of smaller windows. Chiswick embodied this style of the intimate, classical house, dedicated more to art than living, in landscaped grounds on the rim of London. It introduced Palladianism and Venetian style windows where castles had been dominant before. The outcome for Lord Burlington was a familiar, yet noble dwelling place to house friends and family.

This style of house with its less rigid form of sociability became a model. Van Brugh, another notable designer, was

---

[1] F. Young, *The Book of the Scottish Garden*, photographs by Brinsley Burbidge

influential in the mix, and Scotsmen took the classical mode to heart. John Clerk of Penicuik and his son of the same name took trips to England to garner the look of these new country houses and gardens. They and their friends in the Adam family made themselves experts in classical adaptation. In fact, Sir John Clerk of Penicuik wrote a detailed epic in verse on landscape gardening, entitled *The Country Seat*, first published in rhyme in 1727. William Adam made it his 'second bible'; and the two classicists became close friends.

Thus, over the 18th century, landscape design, as it was carried out in practice and theory, became intertwined between England and Scotland. Of course, that did not stop patriotic rivalry, but whichever way it was received, public discussion helped advance the cause. The landscape around grand houses became natural in designed fashion. Lakes and clumps of trees later took over under the influence of 'Capability' Brown, and this naturalness made it inviting to come and discover the house. For us now it seems second nature, but then it was a revolution, doing away with parterres and the overview downwards on an ever-receding countryside. Yester House, in East Lothian, has a picture of its parterres in 1695 by James de Witt which attests to its fashionable gardens seen from the house.[2] It was to be remodelled along natural lines, but as with many grounds, earlier versions survive like palimpsests, still peeking through.

William Adam, friend of Clerk and father to the brothers who caused such a stir in England, deserves his place as one of the first advocates of the natural. He did not always realise his full ambition, but it is evident in most of his work. To quote AA Tait from his seminal study of Scottish landscape gardens in the hundred years from 1735:

> ...Lord President Dundas, a highly successful lawyer, showed most of the props of any formal garden – a bastioned parterre, a wilderness, a great avenue, cascade and basin – all of which derived from the late gardens of Wise and Loudon, or

in Scotland from Bruce and Edward. But in his adaption of
these elements of baroque design, Adam broke with as much
tradition as he followed... Adam proposed at Hopetoun, and
possibly at the Drum and later at Arniston, a more monu-
mental, and at the same time harmonious, termination for
his vistas... He attempted... at Arniston... the bulbous form
of Arthur's Seat, some twelve miles away at the edge of Edinburgh, as the ideal closure for the northern end of the Great
Avenue. This would also have given the house a fleeting
glimpse of the city and brought animation...[3]

In such influential estates, close to the capital city, William
Adam directed the fashionable gaze beyond the garden and connected with landscapes, rural and urban. He brought into the
landscape garden more than the formal reminder of classical
times, as at Chiswick, and instead created an island of reminders,
he opened out a sightline into the goings-on of the city, its surroundings and its seasonal moods. The avenues led back to life
as it was in the outside world. It was not staged, but a natural
vista into Edinburgh and Arthur's Seat, which were far away but
connected.

These visual and social relations which Adam explored had
profound implications. The many meanings embedded in the design of landscape gardens were no longer self-contained. They
were not separate terrains you entered to think; your seeing and
thinking was pushed outwards, to link with the city or other
landmarks that an avenue of trees could frame. The thoughts and
emotions were extended too, as far perhaps as a sea view. The
models were no longer worlds apart into which you could enter
to conserve yourself; they applied to a world beyond the garden
as well. Yet the garden itself had voices that accompanied your
gaze and breathed beside you. They returned you to musings that

[2] AA Tait, *The Landscape Garden in Scotland 1735–1835*, p.66

[3] AA Tait, ibid., p.27

united experiences of past and present, country and city, nature and self, land and sea. The Enlightenment gaze looked out to earn and perhaps acquire.

Landscape gardens of the 18th and early 19th centuries have suffered by their categorisation. Each one, however, evolved in different ways. The essential thing is to personally appreciate the features of each one and how it embellishes what can be seen. It is through direct viewing that these gardens still matter to people – past, present and future.

The early gardens give insight into divinities with virtues to emulate, stories that intrigue and supernatural powers that enhance the natural world and which become accessible in gardens planned for such appreciation. The more 'natural' gardens, given over to expanses of lawn and strategically placed clumps of trees with water in the form of a lake or river, are a departure from the more ornamental features, but they too represent an artificial design, now geared to lingering in restful contemplation. Then the flowerbeds became more prominent, as the eye and heart of the beholder wanted nearer things. The 18th century was approaching the Victorian. The smaller garden was gaining ascendency. Houses of a middling size became more prominent rather than estates. Cottage gardens became favourites and their style infiltrated larger scale grounds.

None of these developments lessened the pleasures of gardening, but increasingly varied approaches were offered. To take just one element out of the many gardens, the close focus rather than the expansion of viewpoints, becomes clearer. Landscape gardens gloried in ornaments of every kind. The Gothic, often attributed a latecomer's role, can be spotted in early gardens too. Painshill, near London on the Mole River, an early landscape garden, sports a Gothic pavilion from which to view the enchantments of the garden. The epitome of the Gothic is Horace Walpole's Strawberry Hill, in which he gathers details he has saved from the medieval through his extensive collecting.

A classical allegory, nymphs adorning a statue of the god Pan.
(© Science Museum / Science and Society Picture Library)

Gothic embellishment then threads its way through the buildings and ornaments of many landscape gardens.

Many options are offered as already evoked. Shimmering temples across lakes take up a theme of the supernatural. Or vistas take the visitor beyond the garden. The variety of near and far is incorporated in landscape gardens. The problem is to appreciate what variety has to offer and to realise the many ways we can be intensely engaged. No matter if these designers were at one with the local countryside or not. Much criticism was made of the parks with too natural a look. Landowners increasingly wanted more powerful motifs, more waterfalls and gorges. 'Capability' Brown was, despite his aligning of clumps of trees and lakes along artificial perspectives, accused of being much too natural. But landscape gardening was there to be much more than manipulated countryside. It was there to evoke, to prod, if you will, the thoughts and emotions of anyone who walked the terrain.

But to pause on such a journey is vital, since the worth of every landscape garden is its capacity to involve the viewer in a time out of time. That might be from the century of its inception to the present day or a moment of infinity. That needs reflection. The more focused we are, whether on the far or near, the more time's relativity is realised and the more distanced today's problems become. The reflective pause becomes therapeutic. It is something that we have inherited for today's gardens of whatever period.

Consider again the virtues of the gods and goddesses these gardens have evoked. Flora, the goddess of vegetation, and only lately of flowers, reminds us of seasonal change. She remains a statue, but in her presence the mind's eye sees not only the unfolding colour of roses and daisies, but the withering of all to brown stalks and mottled leaves as they fall. Ceres pines for her daughter Flora (or Persephone) as winter comes and so do we. The goddesses are with us and so is earthbound Pan. This wicked and fugitive divinity with his goat foot is playing his pipes. He complements Ceres and Flora. As ever there is a plethora of gods hiding as is their wont in the vegetation or rock pools. Pan has the gift of sound in the wind, with his pipes, seen and not seen, so imagined, but also real. This statuary never moves, but landscape gardens bring them in among trees and out of hidden or suddenly revealed temples where they move through the elements and ascend or descend between earth and sky.

The landscape gardens paid tribute to the pagan gods and goddesses. In nature these were the presences that lurked most evidently in the vales and hanging woods of the garden. The gods and goddesses were closely allied to the natural elements. They emerged from forms fashioned by the consciousness of 'natural' designers, but they were couched within a reverence for the immaterial that arose from a reverence for nature herself.

This sense of nature was projected onto the person that took the time and effort to involve herself or himself seriously in the garden experience. These messages so mutely but strongly voiced in the garden are a legacy to the present, allied to poetry, music and painting. The gardens silently enhance the visitor of whatever culture or period. They invest in the visitor and want to provoke us to see more than what is apparently there 'by nature'. That is the value of landscape gardens and why they and their creative inspirations for contemporary gardening still matter.

There is always a third party to the garden and the design. We are the sentient grace that comes into the garden. No garden is plausible without the person that engages with it. The visitor travels. But this movement takes the visual garden inside and makes of it the green place in which emotion, thought and the interchange back and forth between them is fruitful. That is the recompense for each and every person willing to open mind, spirit and soul. We enter the green space and who knows how we slow down and how we benefit from looking, and then leaving again with an altered internal vision, an enlivened humanity.

Landscape and Botanic Gardens

THE GRADUAL DIFFERENTIATION between traditional Herbals and the description of plants as a separate science of botany was made over centuries. The science was aimed at the identification and naming of the various species of plants in order to serve solely botanical needs. The herbal knowledge had primarily a medicinal purpose. Early Herbals were used in treating the ill and the growing of plants in these instances was intended for such applications.

The men, and a few women, who grew and described these plants were usually physicians, picking up from the monastic healers. They had travelled the world. But plants have unpredictable natures, they grow in different places and it takes knowledge to identify them. Word of mouth was used together with written delineation, and these methods were not decisively parted for centuries.

Pictures of plants too were provided, but some were merely copied, and this added to the confusion. Physicians and apprentices had to learn and discern. It was quite a challenge to treat the ill properly. Those renowned for their knowledge added to their reputation by having their Herbals printed. Often, they augmented their wisdom in healing by becoming interested in the new science of plants. For some botany became the primary object, building on the Herbals that had been useful for healing and referencing.

Botany was a science that emerged through its medicinal uses, but then developed as a formal discipline in its own right. Nonetheless, this definition was a product of centuries. There was a back and forth struggle from medieval times into the 18th century. Those in the know had to exercise three qualities. These were first an ability to read Latin as well as the vernacular tongues;

second a willingness to look at plants and recognise them in their real growing habitats; and thirdly, as physicians and healers, the knowledge of how and when to apply their medicinal qualities.

The printed Herbals made the lore of plants more accessible and proved popular. This was, of course, an international trade just as the trade in plants was a wide-ranging geographical exchange. Not everything grew under the same conditions or possessed the necessary qualities. Some plants from the southern hemisphere had to be grown elsewhere under artificial, glasshouse conditions when these were available. Or plants had to be imported, grown and supplied in line with their special needs and conditions. Gardeners were thus much prized as guardians of the natural materials for science and healing.

There were some spurious claims as well, such as the barnacle tree in *Gerard's Herball* of 1597. From this tree near the water, eggs dropped in which barnacle geese were supposedly spawned. Of course, the author of this well-read English Herbal had no personal observations to work from, but he included it in his book. Some traditions continued unchallenged.

Vernacular Herbals were produced in many languages after the printing presses got going. They copied woodcuts and etchings, so only those conversant with books could differentiate the various plants shown. The same was true of their verbal descriptions of plants. Some were copied; some were entirely new according to geographic area. A well-researched book, Agnes Arber's *Herbals*, tells of the entwined intricacy involved in the international production of Herbals from 1470 to 1670 and their slow progress in revealing the botany of plants. Arber calls the way Herbals struggle for an accurate description of plants as 'tacking' towards our knowledge of botany.

There are modern Herbals galore in print today. To begin with, botany shows only how intricate the life of plants can be. But for those absorbed in the ever more challenging knowledge of how plants evolve, how they change under various conditions,

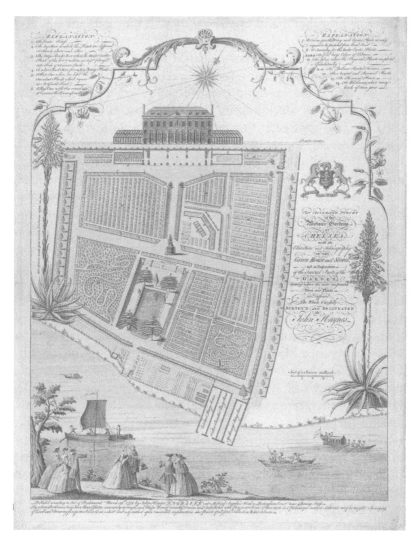

*An illustrated plan of the Chelsea Physic Garden by John Hayes,
1751. (Wellcome Collection. Attribution 4.0 International (CC
BY 4.0))*

where to find them, and even how they fit into gardens of every kind, botany can be all-consuming. In the face of an environmental crisis, botany has become a central scientific discipline of our time, as well as a popular passion.

We know for example that we should cultivate the useful insects which are declining in numbers, especially bees of every sort. We find that each flower is adapted in its own way to attracting insects, some giving within deep throats rewards of pollen for long-tongued insects; others not caring what they attract, especially some of the cow parsley or the giant hogweed species, which will dot any insect with pollen. Here is another area in which science takes precedence over a simple love of colour and texture. But then, we as gardeners have to take ever more fellow creatures into consideration, if we are to extend our observation, planting and love in response to a changing planet. Suddenly gardens matter more than ever.

Physicians and healers were of course aided by the precision of botany as it advanced – it was an interwoven art. Amateurs as well as professionals played a part. In the 18th century Mrs Delany, née Mary Granville, the companion to the wealthy Dowager Duchess of Portland, Margaret Cavendish-Bentinck, did botanical work, pasting and cutting fine specimens. Mrs Delany was innovative as well as creative. These flower specimens, among them the newly imported and thrilling, candelabra-like tiered flowers of the horse chestnut tree from North America, are on display in the British Museum. The more usual herbaria of dried specimens are stored wherever there are botanical gardens.

Aside from dedicated amateurs, which women had to be until the 20th century, medical practice was dependent on knowledge of Herbals and botany. As the British Empire expanded, this included many imports and exports. Scotland exported not only gardeners who acquired detailed know-how of the conditions under which plants thrived – and the basic knowledge of the

plants themselves – but intrepid explorers and collectors in faraway places such as China, Japan and North America. Imports of
trees, leaves and other whole plants increased as the methods of
preserving them on the long sea voyages improved.

Landscape gardens and medicinal gardens are not often com-
pared. Yet both involve the well-being of humans. Both have a
rich history based on international outreach, but they display
their knowledge differently. When landscape gardens emerged in
Britain, Physic or medicinal gardens also continued to develop.
There were connections but the gardens themselves were dissimi-
lar. The early landscape garden was extensive, winding and given
to making lakes integrated with trees, hidden and revealed. They
did not feature much flower planting. This was in contrast to the
detailed records of plant species and genera – developed after
the introduction of the Linnaean system – that the past centuries
invested in the *hortus medicus* or physic garden. They were normally smaller, often enclosed, with intensely cultivated beds of
the plants used in medical teaching.

The contrasting development of both kinds of garden also
reveals connections, above all the mental agility and adaptability
required to orientate toward new plants. North American plants,
as they were introduced, played a vital role in both garden types;
as did later explorations in Asia, particularly in China. Ships
were laden with new and exciting plants, coming both from the
east and west.

The landscape garden had gone beyond the rigid parterres
viewed from windows of châteaux. It loosened their fixed, confined layouts in an expanding terrain. The British landscape garden allowed a relative equality between the nobility and their
visitors, who were encouraged to chance upon scenery and to
meditatively glance outward and inward. The physic garden
sustained more formality and was very strict in observing how
plants grew and their specific application. It placed primary value
on the plants themselves. Its spatial layout was different: the beds

were arranged according to each variety and possible mutations. It was mostly flat, visible to all and measurable.

The first physic garden, or *hortus medicus,* was founded in Padua in 1545, followed a few years later by Pisa, then Leiden in 1590. In 1621 a physic garden was founded in Oxford and then in Chelsea in 1673. Their ancestry goes back to medieval monasteries and the monks' ministry to the sick. The Herbals continued to cite the monastery gardens and their library records of plants with their virtues.

But this new phase was grounded less in a general philosophy of nature and more on specific experiments. The Chelsea Physic Garden shows the interest collectors and herbalists had in a systematic garden. The Physic Garden at Oxford offered the same inclusion and the same order – making way for the Linnaean classification of all plants. Farther north, close by the landscape gardens and the houses created by the Adam family, there was a parallel progression.

John Adam had an acquaintance, John Hope. Both men belonged to prominent families who knew how to deal with the public face of the upper middle classes and the nobility. Hope was the son of a surgeon and then himself Professor of Medicine and Botany at the University of Edinburgh, where he was devoted to his teaching, practice and research. Hope was part of an Enlightenment enterprise based in the city. He belonged to many societies, whose membership comprised of university men, lawyers, clerics and landowners. His networking was potent as he was able to use his connections to bring different aspects of society to bear on advancing common interest. By all accounts Hope was a convivial man, who knew when and how his standing could be used to benefit a cause.

Hope had taken his medical degree at the University of Glasgow in 1750 where he heard the lectures of William Cullen. These were the first in Scotland to introduce the Linnaean system, and Hope learned early on the practical benefit, as well as the

A wood engraving of an original 1750 work by Henry Gillard Glindoni showing men botanising in the Physic Garden at Chelsea near the statue of Sir Hans Sloane. (Wellcome Collection. Attribution 4.0 International (CC BY 4.0))

novelty, of categorizing plants according to a new order. This system classified living organisms into groups depending on their structure and characteristics. He was also taught Dioscorides' *De Materia Medica* by Charles Alston, who was prominent and well researched in the area of treatments and their sources. Hope was consequently well-equipped, socially and educationally, to lead his profession through teaching. But more than that, his life was devoted to his subject.

From his Scottish base Hope joined the prominent teachers in the famous botanical gardens of his time. As Director, or Regius Keeper, of the Royal Botanic Garden Edinburgh, as well as a professor, Hope became crucial to international acceptance

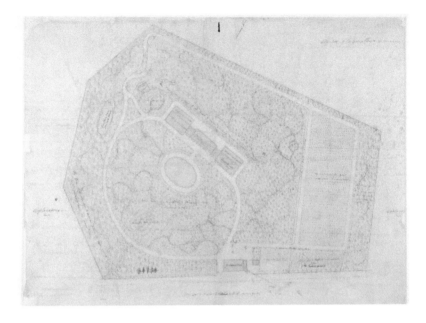

John Hope's Leith Walk garden. (Image courtesy of the Trustees of the Royal Botanic Garden Edinburgh)

of the Linnaean system. During his time as Keeper, Hope oversaw the relocation of the garden from Trinity Hospital to a larger site on Leith Walk. The new garden embodied Hope's vision and was new in two vital aspects. It was built to conclusively articulate the system that Carl Linnaeus had invented. Moreover, it surpassed Oxford and Chelsea by additionally ordering a botanical garden along landscape lines, even using a lopsided hexagon rather than a square in its visual design.

   Instead of the flat arrangement in rows with labels, as in other botanical gardens, Hope's Edinburgh layout offered a more leisurely and enticing way of looking at its materials. The winding walks, although along the families of plants, echo meandering revelations rather than the boxed learning incorporated in earlier gardens. These circuitous walks are key features of landscape gardens: they reveal rather than give an overview all at once. In this way Hope was a leader not only in botanical advances but in adapting the botanical garden to the modern fashion of his day. One could say that Hope introduced the modern botanical garden that we use for learning and recreation today. The garden experience was itself both education and pleasure. To this day the Royal Botanic Garden of Edinburgh builds on this legacy in its greatly enlarged site at Inverleith.

Hope deliberately used his centrality to influential Enlightenment networks to gain support for transforming the *hortus medicus* into a botanical garden. It was still to be primarily a place for educating medical students, but also to be serviceable to the growing public who were attracted by this demonstration of gathered plants in one location. Some men who attended Hope's classes did not take a degree; instead they went on to travel in the still expanding British Empire. They sent observations, seeds and specimens back to Edinburgh because they had become vitally interested in botanical matters. Thus, the networks that Hope built through his students extended worldwide. Those who did go into medicine remained faithful to the practice of botany. But they also focused on dispatching foreign and exotic plants – those that had never previously been cultivated in Britain – and then sent them to the Regius Keeper and Professor.

It is not overstatement to say that Hope placed his new garden concept at the centre of society. He retained close ties across the social classes from aristocrat to gardener – even to architect – through personal acquaintance and professional contact. Another of the Adam family, John eldest son of William, went to school in Dalkeith with John Hope.

The Adam family as previously noted was also deeply involved with the new building of Inveraray Castle, commissioned around 1750, just as Hope was going to University, by Archibald Campbell, 1st Duke of Argyll. The Duke was, until his death in

1761, an early patron of Hope's botanical endeavours and his patronage was taken up by the Duke's cousin, James Stuart, 3rd Earl of Bute.

These aristocratic Scottish dynasties were also politically influential in London. The 3rd Earl of Bute contributed significantly to the makings of a botanical garden at Kew. This site was then a royal holding attached to the White House, a Palladian mansion since pulled down. At first this was the province of the Prince of Wales, Frederick, the son of George II. But he died in 1751. His wife, Princess Augusta, developed an intense love of botany and a friendship with the Earl of Bute. They set up the botanical gardens within her estate, which then attracted contributions through their wide connections, including many travellers. The botanical riches of Kew were, and still are, renowned the world over.

But equally remarkable, though not much noted, was the location of this botanical garden within one of the early landscape gardens which had been fashioned by William Chambers. His revitalising of the White House estate – Kew Gardens to be –involved creating artificial mounds upon which were set temples, columns and most famously a ruined arch. He erected foreign ornamental buildings, notably the Pagoda of several storeys with bells and dragons. This conformed with the ideal of global lands open to the imagination, but also reflected the landscape desire to encounter mythological beings not found in the everyday world. To place science in the midst of this mythic universe was truly an innovative accomplishment. Princess Augusta and the Earl of Bute saw plants and temples as one. They envisioned and built mounds on the flat, Thames-side landscape, upon which their temples to gods, goddesses and the spirit of the wind were erected. They changed the outlook in all senses of the term.

Beyond these classical temples, William Chambers' design called for exotic ornamental buildings, such as the Pagoda, which he enhanced by flanking it, amongst partitioning trees, with a

John Hope. (Image by John Kay. Image courtesy of the Trustees of the Royal Botanic Garden Edinburgh)

Moorish Alhambra and a mosque. These two were taken down later – and the overall design was criticised for containing too many waylaying buildings and for not being natural enough in the sense of 'Capability' Brown. But with his patrons' support, the range of buildings demonstrated that the early landscape garden was a site of broadening experience and encounter. It reached beyond ordinary nature, giving foreign and celestial imaginings room to breathe.

Chambers' ideas were taken up in many gardens, including continental ones, as the fashion for pagodas, tea houses and tea drinking was rife in the 18th century. China itself was far away and inaccessible to most, so these buildings played a vital part in imagining the exotic. William Chambers had built the ten-

A view of the wilderness with the Alhambra, the Pagoda and the mosque at Kew. All except the Pagoda were removed in the 19th century. (Mary Evans Picture Library)

storey octagonal Pagoda in 1761 as part of the royal park. Kew Gardens embraced the concept and spread the desire to erect these ornaments with drooping bells and tiered roofs and ironwork. Also at work was the desire to play-act, to be more than just the mundane self. The garden invited mediations and dreams; it spread imaginings of stepping beyond the immediate restrictions of place or time. This environment became so desirable that it determined the furnishing and decoration of whole rooms inside stately homes, not only the gardens beyond their windows.

In this context, the visit by John Hope in 1766 to England was more than just to see what plants and what exotics he could find in the gardens of Kew and Chelsea. He acquired knowledge from fellow Scots in England, such as the accomplished gardener William Aiton, though this was in regard to plants, not their pleasurable arrangement. It was a fine divide. He was a university man and one used to an urban environment, but he was also aware of the traditions and accelerating developments in landscape gardens.

Hope went, for example, to William Shenstone's garden, The Leasowes. There was, as we described, a connection between this recently designed landscape garden and that of John Adam in Edinburgh in North Merchiston. The visit, and the close affinity between these gardens, is made explicit by Adam, and Hope too mentions his viewing of The Leasowes. He seems to have gone out of his way to see Shenstone's pride and joy. There appears to have been a special regard for this particular early landscape garden on the part of active and thoughtful Scots.

This may have been because the Scots were highly regarded, middle-class men professionals, not landed aristocrats, though linked with key noble patrons. The Leasowes was a much-appreciated model since it was moderately sized and yet exhibited the ornamentation deeply regarded by Adam and Hope. It possessed many and varied buildings on a circuitous walk. But, at the same time, it was manageable and suited to familial gatherings. It also worked as a *ferme ornée* and so providing an income from the agriculturally worked fields. This balance could appeal to canny Scots.

But best of all, The Leasowes provided for an imaginative exploration of classical and Enlightenment knowledge. On the walk – and this was only meant to be in one direction, anticlockwise – disparate items such as a Ruined Priory, Gothic Seat and Virgil's Grove met friends and visitors. William Shenstone was a poet, and a not an overly rich owner. His vision was of the pleasures of the imagination and agreeable sensations on a peripheral, but extensive walk, which allowed visitors time to contemplate the riches of the past, along with associated writers and their influence.

This was powerfully effective because the beauty of the ruin or the grove augmented recollections brought to mind by walking the garden. The garden ornaments, from urns in commemoration to waterfalls and lakes for (melancholy) reflection, were journeys of the mind. His definition of the picturesque, the pictorial, was of a series of views painters might have called to view. The landscape garden evoked the sublime and the beautiful which were very much in vogue. This suited John Adam as the proprietor of North Merchiston House, but more to the point, it amplified the ideas of John Hope, as he wanted to teach botany while delivering his education along curvaceous walks which made his garden pleasurable.

There is good evidence that a significant number of lay people, beyond the Dowager Duchess of Portland and her companion Mrs Mary Delany, were immersed in botany. The chaplain of the Duchess was the Reverend John Lightfoot, to whom she granted special leave to write and research his *Flora Scotica*. Such strong interest in plants and their taxonomy was not just a matter for medical students, it also engaged a discerning and growing public. John Hope knew this. He had asked for the help of the Duchess and her son in buying the Leith Walk plot for his botanical garden. He must have been aware of their botanical interests. He was, of course, not laying out a new landscape garden, though he was using his new botanical garden to effect some of the principles of landscape gardens. He was primarily interested in his medical students and the faculty of medicine. But botany in this guise also meant a wider audience for his work.

This lay interest in planting, and the excitement around cultivating new introductions and exotics, bridges the divide between the landscape and medical gardens. This informed interest, a value placed on plants for their botanic worth as well as their aesthetic properties drove the new era of plant-hunters. These men, and the international networks upon which they relied, changed the nature of both landscape and botanical gardens and drew them closer together.

The Bartrams, John and his son William, were in contact

with Londoners ranging from lowly working gardeners to savants such as Dr John Fothergill and the rich Dowager Duchess of Portland. In his travels to South Carolina and to Florida – territories still wild and unexplored in 1773 – William Bartram discovered many new plants and animals, including birds. He sent illustrations of the botany of American plants to London, while his father sent information from the botanical garden John had established near Philadelphia.

This interchange between the Old World and the New increased as means of transport became more hospitable to plants. The Wardian case is a prime example: it was an almost airtight and humid glass container that was later used in Victorian times for growing ferns. But initially it was prized for keeping plants alive on ships. Such technological innovations multiplied to cope with the many months sailing ships needed at sea before reaching their destination ports. The trade in plants was keenly pursued and it had the effect of recruiting a much larger number of people into the international botanical enterprise.

There were also networks within networks such as the notoriously clannish Scots. Then there were co-religionists – Dr John Fothergill was a Quaker, as was John Bartram. The Quakers included marine merchants such Peter Collinson. All knew each other and together they hugely expanded the trade in seeds. By these routes, North American plants entered London and the British Isles. Archibald Campbell, 3rd Duke of Argyll, certainly planted North American trees in Scotland and some, from his estate at Whitton, were subsequently moved to Kew Gardens. In Perthshire's Dunkeld, the first larch was planted with inestimable consequence not only for estate gardens but the wider Scottish ecology.

John Bartram was appointed King's Botanist in North America and his botanical garden was seen as the first of its kind in the British colonies. It survived the revolution and can be visited to this day in Kingsessing, by the Schuylkill River, north-west of Pennsylvania.

David Douglas, 1836. (Image courtesy of the Trustees of the Royal Botanic Garden Edinburgh)

On both sides of the Atlantic, an avid circle of all classes now wanted exotics in their gardens. Dr Fothergill had his garden in Upton, near London and prided himself on growing plants that almost no one else reared. He represented the close ties of physician and botanist. John Bartram travelled as far as Lake Ontario and to the south-east, including East Florida, in search of specimens to meet the transatlantic demand. William Bartram went further south and east, meeting Native Americans as well as settlers. He recorded his explorations a popular book, *Bartram's Travels*, which came out in 1791. This was an important text for Coleridge and Wordsworth in the emergent Romantic movement which espoused closeness to Nature. Their poetic credos led to a fresh burgeoning and widespread expansion of the landscape movement in the 19th century, which will be discussed in the next chapter.

In the Pacific north-west it was the Scotsman David Douglas who introduced a large number of new specimens. He kept avid journals and his life was anything but tranquil as he pursued new flora and fauna throughout the wilderness. He was the son of a stonemason, and born near Perth. William Jackson Hooker sponsored David Douglas' early career. Douglas was employed as gardener in the Botanical Gardens of the University of Glasgow, where Hooker was the Garden Director and Professor of Botany. Later, Hooker, and then his son, became head of the Royal Botanical Garden at Kew. But before he went to Kew, he took Douglas with him on a botanical expedition to the Scottish Highlands.

The Douglas Fir was named after this intrepid Scotsman, but he discovered many other pines, many of which were transported to Europe, among them the Sugar Loaf Pine. Native Americans climbed the tree and gave him the seeds. Douglas made three journeys to North America in all. He went to the Pacific north-west in 1824 to 1827, and then again in 1829 to the Columbia River, to San Francisco and then to Hawaii. His expedition of 1824 was the most successful. He introduced, among others, the

Sitka Spruce, the Western White Pine and the Ponderosa Pine to the British landscape and its timber industry. He also introduced Penstemon and the California poppy to our gardens.

Another famous botanist of the early 19th century was Robert Fortune, born in 1812 and later employed at the Royal Botanic Garden Edinburgh. He is known for his initiation of the tea trade in China, but his travels also resulted in the cultivation in Europe of many beautiful new flowers and plants. He was admired for his introduction, among others, of peonies, azaleas and chrysanthemums.

Douglas and Fortune are prominent 19th century examples of how botanical knowledge and plant introductions reached a significant international scale and scope. Gardens were open to imports and revelled in planting exotics. Yet the formational centuries were as international as later ones. The pioneering Scottish doctors, Andrew Balfour and Robert Sibbald, who founded the first botanic garden in Edinburgh had met in France and were part of a 17th century community of European learning that took root in their native capital. They leased their first plot near the Abbey at Holyrood in 1670, soon expanding to the garden of Trinity College Hospital, now buried under Waverley Station. When John Hope moved their physic garden to new grounds in 1763, he gave the arrangement of plants a new scientific and cultural purpose. As we have seen, he broadened the focus on medical professionals to an international community of lay people interested in exotic and native plants. But he was building on an earlier tradition of international study.

This phase in the garden story was driven by people combining their knowledge of plants with a passion for their own landscape gardens. Hope tapped into and stimulated this Enlightenment blend of Reason, Emotion and Nature. He made the botanic garden pleasurable, and defining for this new taste, so that people found an intimate joy in walking while gaining knowledge about plants.

Gardens now grew as places of enquiry and psychological nurture. People came to view the plants and enhance their botanical ideas. Then they wanted these plants in their own gardens to enrich form and colour, while advertising their newfound knowledge. It was an important augmentation that the natural landscape garden was only coming to appreciate as the 18th century yielded to the 19th. In more immediate terms, the flowers and exotica of many nations were incorporated into British landscape gardens, where they enhanced the core horticultural experience and added another dimension to the multi-faceted importance of gardening. Science, pleasure and wellbeing walked hand-in-hand into a new era.

The Picturesque and the Countryside

WE MUST NOW re-trace our steps a little in order to throw light on the emergence of the Picturesque and then move forward again into the 19th century when the Romantic movement became a dominant force in garden design.

As we have seen, landscape gardens favoured a focal point that showed the past rather than highlighting the temples which the gods or goddesses might still inhabit. Towards the middle of the 18th century, gardeners left some of these ornamental buildings in place, but they also wanted an outlook that included ruins. Rather than resting satisfied with the beauty given by vistas of the countryside, old castles and ancient abbeys were included, framed by trees in pleasing views. They were picturesque because although in ruins now, they were once mighty, and their survival evoked memory and reflection.

The free-flowing landscape gardens of 18th century Britain were not in that sense picturesque. They were designed to be perceived as natural, yet they were contrived. Their woods, lawns and sightlines were the product of much thought on the part of experts. These designers also knew their shrubs and trees. They worked on the damming of the waters and on enhancing or instigating cascades. Not least they arranged how and where conifers and deciduous trees were to impede or liberate the gaze.

These so-called natural gardens were beneficiaries too of botanical advances. The nurseries supplied select trees or shrubs. Many of these nurserymen-cum-gardeners worked all over the British Isles and included a large proportion of Scotsmen entering the trade in England, usually London. For example, in the 18th century alone, well known gardeners of Scottish decent were Phillip Millar, Thomas Blaikie and William Aiken.

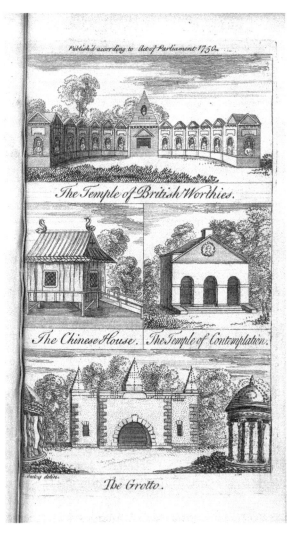

Images and descriptions of the gardens of Viscount Cobham at Stowe in Buckinghamshire in the 18th century including the Grotto and the Temple of Contemplation. (Wellcome Collection. Attribution 4.0 International (CC BY 4.0))

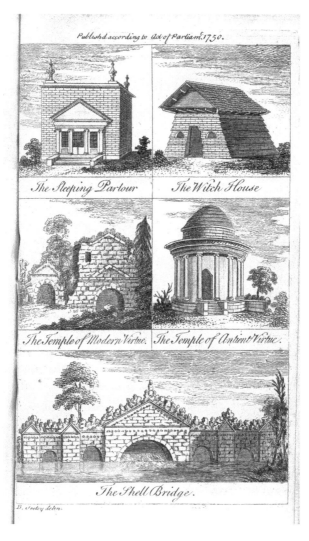

The Sleeping Parlour, the Witch House, the Temple of Modern Virtue, the Temple of Ancient Virtue and the Shell Bridge. (Wellcome Collection. Attribution 4.0 International (CC BY 4.0))

All involved, from nurserymen to landowners, changed the way gardens impacted on visitors. Change was often haphazard. Some kept to the old ways, while others innovated rapidly. Specialists have dated the precise changes, but what concerns us here is the broader impulse. Bringing the countryside into the estate park was definitively practised by William Kent at Rousham, which can be viewed close to its original conception today. The famous garden at Stowe had ornamental buildings which were ruinous, especially the Temple of Modern Virtues. It was meant to be that way and the ruins were, even at the time, a modern construct. Even in older landscape gardens, traces of more modern innovations can be found.

What becomes important is the shift away from invoking Greek gods or classical Rome to put feelings at the heart of the matter. Emotions and thought were engaged by the ruins and their contemplation. From the middle and to the end of the 18th century this was the sought-after state of mind; emotion was gaining ascendancy. British landscape gardens had ruins as a focal point. The intention was to induce contemplative reactions. So the landscape was not just assembled as an inventory of astounding and sentimental pictures, but as a tapestry of emotional reactions to the features toward which your sightline was directed.

Central to this, not least in Scotland, were castle ruins such as Kilchurn Castle on Loch Awe near Oban; Dunstaffnage and Dunolllie Castles; Castle Stalker in Cowal; and many more. They are certainly authentic relics from the past. Near Edinburgh we might name Craigmillar Castle; Craigcrook in Edinburgh, Dirleton and Dunbar Castles in East Lothian; and Linlithgow Palace to the west. These castles have a life of their own. They are not dependent for their effect on the sight of woods, views over lakes or being part of a landscape garden.

But if you view the castles in a designed landscape, they are then deliberately placed to unite past and present. Of course, this is the art of the landscape gardener, but it depends on our parallel response, which is why the change of sensibility this involved came through literature, painting and music as well as garden designs. These ruins become time relative – they bring the historically distant view, of say chivalry or past barbarity, to the window or to the perspective at the end of a pathway of trees. They are a glimpsed as the viewer walks or looks in their direction. They combine the state of the now with the history of the buildings, so generating a sharper awareness of time passing. This in turn leads to inward reflections.

Melancholy was the mood this induced in the 18th century. It was good, our ancestors believed, to bring to mind the deeds and aspirations of the past and to think on the good and the tragic events that had befallen over time. This combination of feelings and mood, of reflection and contemplation, heightened the experience of the garden. It brings home to us that the landscape garden is more than roaming through trees, passing lawns, lochs or waterworks. It educates viewers in the realms of history and the supernatural. It also links thoughts of the present day with experiences of the past to be recalled and anchored once more in our relatively short lives.

These ruminations were often of a distancing sort, causing each person to reassess their approach to difficulties in the here and now. In that Romantic period at the turn of the 18th to the 19th centuries, many writers, foremost Sir Walter Scott, turned to the historical novel. It was not just a nostalgic trip, but one that contained lessons for the present. The gardens, equally, were not just idyllic resorts that wheeled out something that rendered the past innocuous. Burgeoning Romanticism had a sting in the tail. It balanced what was sometimes viewed as the plucky past with the amorphous or even decaying present. Now, it was the reader who made the judgment. Just as in the landscape garden, the user of the circuitous walk was never without confrontations that evoked wonderment and thought. The scenes prompted a pause for reflection – and then a reaction that might be emotionally mixed. The 19th century was increasingly conflicted, which became a troubling source of emotion. Such responses do not swell up from nowhere.

Often enclosed 'pictures' were there to induce sadness or triumph. Such were the scenes of ruined abbeys, which might be sad in their ivy-covered walls or a matter of triumph for devout Protestants. In creating these ruins, the Reformation had realised its aims. The might of the Roman Church had been brought low. But this could be extended to more metaphorical 'ruined choirs' of which only vestiges were left. A contemplation of the past brought Scottish rebellions to mind, or they brought the elegiac wisdom of the Bible home: 'and the mighty shall be brought low.' Others again wondered if the triumph of Protestantism had led to a materialistic age. The Oxford Movement arose to revive the medieval spirit and there was a Roman Catholic renaissance in Britain. The leader of this movement, the recently sanctified Cardinal John Henry Newman, ascribed his inspiration to Sir Walter Scott and to Scott's house at Abbotsford which he often visited.

Ruins, whether fake or real, graced many Scottish and English gardens. Generally, they were placed on heights. Their contemplation brought the Gothic into its own. Ruins were augmented, by additional Gothic arches or ivy growing on arches still intact. The idea was to create places where you could gaze at the fallen past. Many incorporated ruined abbeys which had only arches and skeleton windows left. If they were not too large, they could be placed on a rising crest to walk up, inviting close inspection. A Gothic arch was added sometimes, in this case to heighten a tension with the classical or to evoke long lost habitations in the countryside. These symbolic stones were focal points, though meant as remnants. As the visitor strode to them or saw a scene laid out before a castle or arch, the enclosing tableau was there to raise melancholy thoughts relating the past to the present. The ruin might be Gothic in every sense, causing

The ruins of Fountains Abbey form a focal point in the gardens at Studley Royal, Yorkshire, seat of William Aislabie Esq. (Mary Evans Picture Library)

you to shudder at the decay of once thriving human achievements.

Follies of all kinds, many of them Gothic, populated the Romantic landscape gardens. These eye-catching structures are not just ornamental or picturesque; they further a mood of serious contemplation. They exhibit a purposely decrepit and fallen state. Their ruinous appearance is a monument to time, the remorseless consumer of all human endeavour. These are invariably Romantic imaginings, as the 18th moves into the 19th century. None of the later landscape gardens would be complete if they did not try to match the view with its viewers' sensibilities. Such evocations of history, the nation's past, its great writers and mythical figures animate impressive monuments, sudden visual presentations and disturbing encounters with ruined chapels, temples and obelisks.

In Scotland, the resounding note, if not keening knell, is for the Caledonian Ossian, to whom places are often dedicated. He is the re-imagined bard whose ancient poetry resounded through James MacPherson's Romantic re-inventions across Europe. People who came to Scotland sought landscapes connected to his name. The wilder reaches of rivers with tumbling cascades and rushing water such as at Dunkeld Hermitage, were given associations with him and their romantic nature was doubly enhanced.

These rippling and foaming rivers and burns came to prominence in Romantic gardens. Paths led to where they would be appreciated most. Dunkeld had mirrors that reflected the waters in vivid green or red. This enhancement meant a wild scene was even more memorable through the colours and sounds produced. When you arrived at the pinnacle, overlooking water running its wild race downward, one could marvel at the scenic drama. The rocky path upward and the glimpse over trees and precipice was sure to excite the emotions. Many were the bald rocks and stony outcrops with cascading water in Scotland, all crying out for the presence of a stirring Celtic past.

Robert Adam designed castles that were the new expression of Romantic living. He gave them ruined arches and long receding perspectives past for which you had to cross stone bridges and traverse woods. Culzean Castle is one of his foremost creations. It had no actual medieval past but looked its part better than any ancient tower of defence. The location was ideal, on the rocky coast of Ayrshire, dropping precipitously down to the sea. The landscape gardens he created were old style too, with the castle looking down over terraced grounds. But the wider landscaped gardens were a riot of colour true to the dawning Romantic era of the 19th century.

Adam loved to place his fantastical castles in the raw scenery of Scotland. Together they lent each place added antiquity and showed the wilder woodlands and hills to be the perfect accompaniment. The combination provoked a feeling of continuity with a venerable past, a kind of immortality within the march of time. Adam invites everyone into the gaze of centuries past and, rather than a ruin, he brings us into the medieval experience. Like Sir Walter Scott, Robert Adam avows the Scottish past and brings it within reach of a broad, appreciative public.

Thus a mélange of visual sensations, cultural allusions, architecture and constructed gardens brought the past alive again. How to react, was a personal matter of mood, disposition and curiosity. Some garden writers have claimed that suburban and city gardens hark back to the intimacy created by enclosed medieval gardens so many centuries ago. Your own garden may reflect that small space and you may have favourite colours and the loved plants that produce them. As a garden city, Edinburgh retains its medieval and 17th century walled gardens in the Old Town and the classical ideal of 'countryside in the city' in its Georgian New Town. There is continuing value in the closeness and enhanced attention this usually entails. But exploring the extensive landscape of the Romantic garden holds out adventures of a different sort.

Abbotsford, the baronial castle that Sir Walter Scott created for himself in the Scottish Borders in the early 19th century, confronts us with a much longer history. The building is awash with turrets and the rooms are filled with mementoes of the Scottish past. In doing so Scott calls up many episodes we may have missed and invents many more. His walled gardens are prickly with flowers and colours. Scott's is a picture of the past – and yet it is a moment in time that resounds in different ways. The gardens were new for the 1800s. The many trees Scott planted added to the meditative walks. This otherworld helped him compose and relax. Abbotsford embodied the imagined worlds of his poetry and prose.

Visitors project onto Abbotsford their feelings upon entering a preserved world born of Scottish history and its associated bardic minstrelsy. Abbotsford envelops the visitor in its unique and sometimes strange universe. Robert Adam does this too at Culzean, but once removed. His is a fanciful projection, thought

ABBOTSFORD—THE GARDEN FRONT

Abbotsford, the home and creation of Sir Walter Scott, viewed from the front through the garden. (Mary Evans Picture Library)

out on paper, transcribed into stone, built as a castle and gardens. The owners for whom he worked also added, like Scott, flowers in staggering colours and wide beds. Harking to Scottish centuries past is balanced by walled gardens of brilliant hue. It is the past and present intermingled.

Gardens become good places to test identity. Aspiring to be one thing or another, we look around. What better than the silence of tree-lined walks or walled gardens to weigh up the ground we hope or are willing to tread upon? The tree framed, and consciously opened panoramas, are extensions. They will us to connect to scenes that challenge. This becomes evident when an unknown past suddenly springs to life in the picturesque and we pursue its meaning. For us, it might be a glimpse of past centuries which deepen our understanding of the present. But for Scott Abbotsford is not an imagined alternative; it a vital necessity, a much-needed dose of reality to set against the rationalistic doldrums and materialistic down drag of Scotland's industrial

An engraving of Yester House in 1821.

growth. In his novels, Scott is conflicted between Enlightenment reason and Romantic emotion, but at Abbotsford his inner allegiance is writ large for all to see. He has realised his own ideal refuge and retreat.

Romantic landscape gardens continue to provide enough space and diversion, in their ornamentation and sightlines to inspire our reflections. On a personal level, for example, I went into the now wild avenue of Yester House in East Lothian, full of mature evergreens and deciduous trees. Beeches of that gorgeous hue of yellow and velvet brown laced the avenue, but I could still see it leading to the bridge and then the bald, silvery stones of the house. Inevitably, I reflected and meditated on the fate of the many generations that had lived there. For me, this physical location became something unreal, something contained in a book which I could wonder about, or a dream I might interpret. Overgrown trees bowing in the long avenue of approach and the distant stone bridge and the sight of the ancient house.

We should not disregard these pictures, even though we are not used to seeing them, except on paper or canvas. The views in landscape gardens are meant to broaden horizons and to remind us of the past. And they still function in this way, because part of the picture is you. Standing right there, you are no longer observer only, but included. Perspectives alter as you move; angles increase or recede. As the ruin, castle or ancient building changes, so too does the emotion – you cannot remain uninvolved. We are part of the evolving story.

Waterfalls are meant to be approached the same way. As they are incorporated in the landscape garden, they are framed as far away, then come to be close at hand. This intriguing 'now you see it, now you don't' approach lets you be involved. The sound of rushing water engages the senses. The natural cascade then comes into sight – or is hidden for a time. The Romantic garden plays upon its visitors with this near and far sighting. The sound of water is intriguing. It is hidden in a dell and then revealed as nearby, demonstrating nature's immediate force.

This kind of dell is part of the newly 'wild' garden as it was reinvented towards the end of the 18th century. Especially in Scotland, tumbling burns and bridges of stone rimmed with tossing, native bushes became fashionable. It raised the effect of 'wild' countryside in which winding paths led to Gothic-enhanced homes. Dells multiplied and remain attractive walks. Yet a fine balance was retained between what seemed wild and led to these views and the thoughts they evoked. Many of Edinburgh's most popular nature walks today, along the Water of Leith or the Braidburn owe their origins to these designed dells.

The countryside was taken into the park by more than just seeing a vista far in the distance to contemplate. It was more than a visual extension. Ruins, Gothic arches, stone bridges over wild running burns, hills with cascades through them where water was white in its falling, woods that revealed and hid, but were mostly planted, lochs and rivers taken to be scenery in the landscape garden, all of these were presented as part of the immersive spectacle. They gave the landscape garden something of the flavour of theatre.

The drama of the garden is never to be underestimated. Suggestions of scenes and the insurgence of wildness, be it of nature or the past and history, is what the landscape garden did successfully until the mid-19th century. Then colourful flowers took over, as did a desire to look more closely at what planting in herbaceous borders could achieve. The flower garden began to invade the large garden given over to views and surprise ornaments. Colour and the sequence of height and seasonal growth took the far view to the close-up. The long-century of the Picturesque and the Romantic landscape garden was coming to a natural end.

CONVERSATION
IN A GARDEN
Donald Smith
with
Joanna Geyer-Kordesch

Conversation in the Garden

We spent such a long time creating order in the garden,
now the wind has so easily created turmoil.
From the diary of Joanna Geyer-Kordesch

REACHING BACK THROUGH the centuries, *Why Gardens Matter* shows
how richly layered and textured our contemporary response to both
making and enjoying gardens has become. It brings a lifetime of study
and personal experience together to show the many ways in which
gardens matter to all of us. But the book is also a biographical
journey.

Though she wears her learning lightly, Joanna Geyer-Kordesch has had a distinguished academic career bridging the disciplines of history of medicine and cultural history. After direct-
ing The Wellcome Unit for the History of Medicine at Glasgow
University she became Professor of European Natural History
and Medicine at that University where, after retiring in 2006, she
remains a Professor Emerita.

However, this tale of academic distinction is also a cultural journey. The Kordesch family left Vienna for the USA in the
wake of World War II. Her father, Professor Karl Kordesch, was
a prominent research electro-chemist whose major work was on
rechargeable batteries and fuel cells including the fuel cells that
powered the Apollo Project Command Module. Joanna drove
his home-built hydrogen fuelled electric car in 1970. Her mother
taught children in hospital, both to keep them learning and to interest them in nature. She taught the 'Secrets of Trees', including
all kinds of information about how leaves emerged, how differ-

ent trees had different leaves and their individual fruits. This botanical knowledge was packed into exciting tales and surprising revelations. As Joanna later recalled:

> My visits to botanical gardens all over Europe were first inspired by her – she would hunt them out whatever city she was in. I remember vividly how I was scratched by a very thorny plant, some luxurious exotic overgrowing the path in a glasshouse, as I followed her example! Botanical gardens have a long history in our family. In fact, one of the first exact plant books – with stories about plants included – and one of the first written by a woman, was authored by Aglaia von Enderes, an ancestor of mine. She was Viennese and wrote in German.

Joanna returned to Europe for a school year and then increasing aspects of her University education. By sustaining her bilingualism, the young researcher founded her work on a common European heritage.

So, alongside the lifetime's research on which *Why Gardens Matter* draws, this book is deeply personal. It reflects Joanna's rediscovery in later life of a creative inheritance, in poetry, art and narrative. From 2010 she began to publish her own illuminated poems of nature, under her married name, Joanna Paterson, signifying that it is in Scotland that these two complementary streams have come together.

Based in Argyll and now in East Lothian, Joanna formed an association with the Scottish Storytelling Centre in Edinburgh and its International Storytelling Festival and, by extension, with myself.

In October 2012, in the midst of a series of events relating to the importance of gardens, Joanna suffered a devastating stroke. Her work ceased and she dedicated herself to the rehabilitation process. For a time, I looked after the projects on which we had embarked. I soon realised the extent to which the garden and its importance to our human experience, had become the central aspect of Joanna's life. Her diaries, undertaken with the intent of learning to write, draw and paint again with her opposite hand, show how her garden and its seasonal changes marked the rhythm of her recovery. New shoots emerged alongside triumphs of will and efforts of painstaking patience; periods of dormancy and disappointment converged with frosts and dissatisfaction with winter glooms.

The rhythm of nature allowed Joanna to approach this new period of her life from a different perspective. Her left hand penned a new set of ideas and newly considered ways in which gardens can matter to us, not merely from a historical perspective but from an emotional, creative and truly personal one too.

Despite the after-effects of her stroke, Joanna fought back to recover her cognitive and creative faculties while adapting to physical restrictions. A documentary film 'Stories and Cures', produced by the Scottish International Storytelling Festival, encapsulates this period of struggle and recovery. 'Stories and Cures' was shot in a small suburban garden, for it was during this period that Joanna turned again to gardens as places of meditation and healing. She began to re-apply her academic knowledge to inform her experience and, even more, her new experience to cast fresh light on her life of learning. The cultural phenomena explored by Professor Geyer-Kordesch became in their simplest and most accessible forms a personal necessity and lifeline.

As Joanna progressed in her recovery, she and her husband Jim Paterson moved to East Lothian, where their garden by the River Tyne became the laboratory of her fresh creative endeavours and the crucible of new reflections. I visited Joanna in her garden one summer afternoon. Our conversation evokes her remarkable philosophy of gardens, her deep knowledge of garden history and shows how her experience of the natural world has nourished a healing journey

ॐ ॐ ॐ

Donald Smith: Joanna, we are sitting in your beautiful garden. Is this a good place to have a conversation?

Joanna Geyer-Kordesch: Here in my own garden surrounded by flowers, mainly roses, shrubs and trees with their green leaves now fully out, the world seems unchangeable and filled to the brim with goodness. But, contrary to assumptions, this restful scene is changeable and exciting. What begins as a few green leaves or spears breaking the ground soon shoots upwards and roars into the beauty of buds and flowers. So you are able to sit here watching and each moment is different, it comes as free flowing as any good conversation.

Would you like your book to develop as a kind of conversation with your readers?

I like conversations with plants and people alike. They can be creative and supportive, halting or useful. The silence of plants does not mean they don't abide in your thoughts. You can use them creatively, or just contemplate how cycles function: the winter meditation that goes deep and has no visible signs, or the summer's flourishing growth that is so abundant, rampant even. This book is an invitation to join that conversation. It should encourage readers to browse and learn what the history of gardens has to offer them. It invites the reader to see and, if possible, to walk the gardens themselves.

Gardens began as places to grow food – kailyards, as they were called in Scotland. Is that still important, as in, for example, the community garden movement?

Gardens most certainly began as places to grow food, but as the centuries have gone on they have become spaces for expression.

They are places in which to sit under trees, places to grow roses, or violets to smell or primulas for early colour. Flowers and flowering trees gather scent and in its sweetness you can meditate and be at peace.

In the course of the centuries the kitchen garden was separated from the Picturesque garden. But there is no doubt that vegetables, fruit and medicinal gardens had their roles early in history. This role played by gardens is enjoying a renewal by way of the stress placed on healthy eating today. Growing your own fare has become important. Community gardens are vital to this. The nice thing about today is that we can choose how and what to grow.

What you make space for and grow in your own garden has incomparable health benefits. There are obvious ones like picking fruit or vegetables whenever they are ripe; and don't forget how the exercise of digging and hoeing benefits you. But the mind and emotions are also vital to health – I think there is always a mind-body unity. If you can appreciate what grows, you are already 'outside' yourself and engaged in watching the vegetables or flowers, and you can internalise what happens in this process. It is not one thing but a progression – you learn how to enjoy paying attention. Plants move slowly – they slow you down from the demanding, fast world we are used to today. This slowing down shows us time in another way: you can heal and think things out in your own time. This is health, not in the dimension of 'proper food' alone, but of wholesomeness, integrating body and mind.

Indeed, the Garden of Eden was not about healthy – or even unhealthy eating! Why are gardens places of beauty in cultures across the world?

A good friend of mine once said there is no colour clash in gardens, you can bunch any flowers in a vase, or growing next to each other. Beauty is actually peace of mind – walking and seeing. The diversity in historical gardens emphasises the many differing layouts that brought thoughts or experiences of importance to mind. The Picturesque was just that – scenes of nature so enhanced that trees and lakes and hills impressed you with their beauty. The randomness of nature was suddenly composed. It is like a theatre with themes you should notice. Gardens provide beauty which can enter the soul – they are memorable, such as the vibrant red of a flower or the cascading of waterfalls carefully judged to enhance the sound. Garden beauty is around you. You can sit and imbibe it. And sitting there you become beautiful. You become beautiful in the midst of flowers because there are no rigid preconceived notions. You can become a magical unicorn and your imagination leaves you dancing. A more conventional spot would reduce you to nothing.

But gardens also encourage active creativity. Each plant offers possibilities to the healthy and disabled alike. This goes beyond caring for how and what plants are – even concentrating on an exciting trial of new flowers or vegetables. Experimenting with drawing or painting the garden elicits several advantages. Flowers are notorious for brief spans of beauty. You can expand these and record and remember your interaction. But you develop dexterity of hand, heart and soul. It was this desire that enabled me to write and paint with my left hand after a lifetime of being right-handed. It's horrible at first and then, suddenly, it works.

Gardens are refreshing. Whether you plant one, or paint one or recall what is in one, you heighten your vision, you develop and you concentrate your talent. I could have despaired, but gardens lifted me beyond myself. I was happy to record trees in wavy lines.

Gardens are full of natural cycles such as the growth of plants and the changing seasons. Are these important for people as well?

Gardens are both cyclical and changeable. I think of them as benign mirrors. They reflect how people change in a lifetime, how they continue and how gifted they can be. A plant can go some time – for seasons even – without producing anything, yet suddenly it flourishes. Innumerable courgettes or rose buds will appear and yet in some years the courgette plant produces nothing. So you try again.

And it is important to think about winter. Plants lose leaves, they go brown, they go underground. In a period of hiding, we believe we see emptiness, unproductive withering and plants disappearing from above the soil. Winter desolation ensues. This should be a sign to people that patches of desolation, of perhaps doing nothing, are vital. We need these reversals to grow again, to green the new shoots. To cultivate new insights and ideas like unsheathing new leaves. These may be small – but who cares what size they are? This is our own spring.

Did suffering such a severe stroke lastingly change your sense of gardens? Is that part of how you have changed?

Endurance and a fierce notion about your own path forward, these are the first two virtues to pack into the bag strapped on your shoulder. And never forget laughter as a musical accompaniment. It took me about two years to contain the huge scribbling of my left hand as I switched over from what had been the elegant, small writing I used to do with my right. After my stroke I thought I would be no more than a lumpy sack of potatoes, doomed forever to do nothing but wear an empty smile. Now that smile has substance and encompasses my own judgement on whether my paintings are good or bad. And I don't throw away the bad ones because I learn from them.

A stroke is like a flash of lightning. And it doesn't choose whether it strikes right or left. Mine was a haemorrhage in the brain, leaving the right side of my body without any feeling, the leg and the hand. At first it wouldn't let me stand, nor draw or write. I still totter now, even when walking supported from a railing outside the wheelchair. But the rest of me lets me record, visualise, find the exact placing of lines that I need – for flower stems, for example, when painting. Having the left side intact did not mean my left hand could write or paint. I had to be persistent in training it. Throughout most of my life, I had used my right hand. In this predicament I tried turning to the imaginative whenever I felt low and I was, and continue to be, inspired by my garden.

There is nothing like the quiet companionship of plants to deflect any kind of misery. Think of the slow growth of trees, or what careful deliberation it takes to select the right flowers to plant, and you will learn the patience needed. In what other place can you watch flowers or treetops dance and meet bending green grasses and blue skies? In what other place can you lose yourself in peaceful meditation, even lose yourself and whatever ails you? Where else is the red-into-white curl of a rose petal of great significance? Where else can you say you lost count of time and your problems paled into the yellow of the sunflowers or the intricate nature of ferns? Deal with stress by walking or wheelchairing in a garden and it will revive you. The garden with plants galore and its changing seasons will simply say: 'this small problem is surmountable!'

I can't stress enough the variety that you can notice when involved with those quietly growing things. Stretching beyond physical impairment lets the mind grow. Observation brings the artistic eye to life. Take a rose, for example, and watch it sprouting leaves, then flowering, then casting its leaves off. In just these three actions there are myriad visual notes – written, or pencilled or even in abstract – that you could set down. Even before those splendid, singular, multi-hued, bursting, radiant petals do a dancing show, the thorn-filled stems and ridged leaves culminate in their geometric shapes and there you can also document, even in winter's bareness. It is worth noting how 'nothingness' has its own shapes, how thorns and spare limbs gain shape, curled fingertips taste the cold air. They all give you a picture you can paint in natural winter colours, or you can go wild and render it blue or a stalwart brown, adorning the brown with silver.

What I am saying is: be as free as a child and let that rose be a sparse stem with thorns, just a dark charcoal line, just like winter. Later on in the season, let that rose fascinate in its watercolour wet-in-wet depiction, make it a never-only-one-hue petal glory. And then, days having gone by for half a week or a week, let it float down to the ground limpid, slightly blotched, with cast-off petals on the green grass or the brown soil. Observing only even a single plant gives you – the attentive watcher – the ability to be with the rose and how it lives.

After which you can decide what lines, what medium, what thoughts, will give you a picture of your rose. And if anyone says, 'this is not a rose', you reply 'but you have no idea how complicated roses are and I'm the one who is closest to this rose's life'. The more you look, the more you gain.

Seasonal passages create watchfulness all their own. As a result of your special requirements you can be restricted by cold or heat. Someone will help you wear the right clothes for warmth, or eliminate the cardigan, or bring you a pencil or watercolour tubes and a jar. A mess is another way of meeting interesting people. I found I was dependent, asking for this and that, but in gratitude I donated the painting or got it framed for a friend. You might get a thank-you note as you progress with your art and learn to treasure it!

Creativity when disabled depends on which medium you would like to use or is the best you can manage. Essentially, disability is manageable. Creativity, to my mind, can develop like the tree of life underneath the soil. Tree roots are extensive and they reach out continuously. It may not be seen at first and is very good at hiding. But it signifies steadfastness. Dips in mood can happen – but they can't overcome stalwartness. It may take years, but inching forward has gains – and who knows, an inventive style of new abstraction may result. Gardens, and the marks you make, of every sort, have a way of uniting. What they need is you. Then the garden can flourish on its own, producing plants true to its kind but stirring the imagination.

The gifts gardens harbour for people – and remember, one in five are disabled in some way – benefit everyone in the community that engages with them. Community gardens, or allotments, bring discussions and considerations of what and where to plant. Digging around also means talking and thinking hard. For the disabled it means recognition. To be enabled to participate can have an effect. You are brought into the discussion as a reflective, thinking person. And the help you need, for example on how to manipulate a wheelchair on gravel, aids not only how you approach planting, but also how people see you and can assist you. You are helpless in some ways; but knowledgeable in others. The voice you have is not always a whisper.

One-handed, this last summer I learned something new. I learned how to use the left hand, one-handed, to spray life-giving water – the plants needed it. Raised beds are marvellous for herbs. Robins come close to hop around your wheelchair when they get used to you. They only pretend they are looking for bird food. They like good company.

Last but not least, our health is better the more we breathe fresh air. We get more ideas and go outside. In the late autumn I spin around the house in my wheelchair to see if, finally, the Echinacea, flowers with petals like a daisy, have come up and are displaying their colours. They are only evident in late summer, but given the garden is mostly mature green, they dot it with spots of red in various hues or pure white. Most other plants don't want to bloom anymore.

My Echinacea plants are called 'Tomato Soup' and freshen up green upon green varied leaf offerings with a strident reddish tinged orange. I survey the scene, resting my eyes on these reddish wheels with pointed spokes flowering vividly.

Talking in the garden seems to be very easy. Can we make friends in the garden and improve relationships?

There is a common interest and views to share in a garden. Gardens are friendly places and strangers can ask about the flowers or plants. And that's even better when you are part of a group come to see a historical garden – advice, observation, clarity should be shared! Gardens start people talking, sharing stories and advice, such as where plants grow best, in sun or shade, what mulch to use, or whether wet or dry soil helps the garden plant, but also about layout and placement. I plant close, clematis and roses intertwine. The peonies get a section of their own and their vivid petals in translucent white or deep red, teeth as jagged as chewing the heavens, leave me in awe.

But working in a garden also brings people together without chit-chat. Everyone is accepted as part of a common task. I think that is why community gardens appeal to so many people who find other ways of socialising difficult.

Do gardens give us a sense of belonging in this world? A sense of identity?

Gardens stay put and give what they are given. My mother used to say that in the first year plants sleep, then they creep and in the third year they leap! We belong in this world democratically, no matter if we are a prospering thistle or a diverse geranium. Roses bloom now from June until the first frost. Or you can identify with a dandelion and switch from golden sun-struck circles to wispy white wind-swept wanderer. Apple trees are first full of dainty pink and white blossom, then heavy with fruit.

Gardens bear all kinds of fruit – identity is what we share

– peaches and cream, squashes in autumn, rosemary to garnish, herbs for lovely tea, honeysuckle for the smell. Eating and thinking and drinking teas, gardens invite us in, they are nature made over and we can be grateful that we can throw our very identities to the wind as we become lovers of our second nature.

PART TWO
CREATIVE GARDENS

Gardens in the Mind

GARDENS ARE PLACES designed to help you think and feel. They are physical but can also become spaces within ourselves, because of the relationships between people and plants, rhythms of growth and healing and a slow, gentle sense of time.

Gardens can take any shape or structure and dealing with their diversity opens many options for our approach. From nursing one or two plants of individual choice to walking in an historic garden, the possibilities seem infinite.

All choices, however, mean one thing, an interchange between the person and a quiet growing thing which has a life of its own. Whether the plant is on a windowsill or part of a large and thought-out design, the tree, shrub, flower or vegetable – or weed – will grow. We influence it by providing good soil, light and shade, fertiliser and other nutrients. Or we forget and the plant grows willy-nilly. Either way, the plant interacts with us, and the language is a silent one. Sometimes we 'read' the wants of a plant by how it juts out leaves and even how it grows its buds into flowers. It looks to our care and we throw repeated looks to see how we are progressing. This silent language is how we care. And we know that we and the plant can grow together as well as speak to one another.

That is not to say nothing will change. The seasons and growth vary. So do the nurseries, as they display ever more breeding variations, for example, roses, cyclamen, pansies, violas and a series of other cherished plants. But plants are not objects that lurk unwanted until they have been rediscovered in some dark closet to be resurrected or thrown in the rubbish bin. The plant you like will depend on you and thrive or wither, depending on your knowledge, your affection or your forgetfulness. Plants speak a language unobtrusive but unmistakable.

Instead of telling you about each plant, let me focus on the relationships. This is not about letting the plant grow in optimal conditions, but rather, easing into a bond that never remains static. I have planted Heleniums, for example, in a bed that is for late summer. In November they have become dank and brown buttons still sticking upwards in a wobbly row. Around them are late Japonicas in white and pink, producing pale blooms and turning a face or two or three towards my inquisitive look. Then there are spent roses and other roses with a bloom or several late buds when I have given up hope.

I ask this or that person in the know how to keep each of them going. This builds a network of helpful people and concerned friends. Even people far way engage with each other in letters about the plot of ground you have and if you are trying out different plants to grow. It becomes an adventure. You become cantankerous or welcoming to others as well as to your leafy friends.

Any piece of soil will do to make a beginning. Any book will do to help. And then you can widen the scope. Mute conversations will ensue and they build inside you. That thing of sticks will unfurl a leaf and you will greet it. I was faced with a wisteria about which I knew nothing – a sinuous set of stems unfolding towards the roof and doing its best to block the gutters. I read an appropriate magazine and took advice and cut the growth back. The wisteria decided to love my treatment, developing even more pendulous leafy, sinuous windings. The flowers were few, but the many leaves and snake-like filaments shaded the sitting room. It still blocks the gutters, but I have a new relationship with wisteria.

Creativity hides in how we react to the other living thing – plants have the advantage of silence and growing in their season. When viewed in other people's gardens they lead to a number of thoughts. We are attracted or repulsed. It is helpful to go to different places and see how we can think and learn. The past has thoughts to offer. And this is how we come to visit gardens around our home, and if we wish it, further afield. These gardens are attuned to the needs of times past, but as we have traced in Part One they build a sequence. Not only that, but their inventions are trailed over time, so that some overlap with our present while some are out of fashion when we look back at them. None is lost to our present enjoyment.

Topiary is an instance. When in the very early 18th century landscape architects gazed at gardens heavy with sculptured artefacts formed from evergreen trees, they closed their eyes in dismay and criticism. More than that, writers such as Alexander Pope and Stephan Switzer found much to say about how humans distorted trees out of their natural shapes. These leading writers both regretted the work that created balls, crowns, peacocks, pyramids and other elaborations in Renaissance gardens. Joseph Addison wrote with great pleasure of his natural garden where all manner of plants sprung from the ground without external shaping. He made the point that he did not like the artificial.

The gardens these pioneers went on to found were memorials of the past in different ways and innovative at the same time. They were personal to the people they commemorated. Pope, for example, thought of his mother when he erected an obelisk in his garden by the Thames River. Then he made a grotto of stones he had gathered there, as an expression of self. He wrote and reflected on the joys of water and the pleasant sound of its descent in his grotto. It was the natural world and yet it was not the natural world. Topiary was done away with by savage criticism, but in the 19th century, and in more recent times, it has gained favour again, especially in cottage gardens.

What Addison, Pope and Switzer hoped for was to turn gardens from a noble setting and highly stylised courtly pleasure, to a place where many paths meandered so it would delight writers, the middle classes and the libertarian Whigs. This, as we have outlined, was a historic enterprise. But the creativity involved is still open to us today.

On a grand scale landscape gardens were only done by aristocrats of means. But while they took it upon themselves or ordered someone else to design the landscape garden, they often had visitors who came to see what was done – even when they were absent and had a subordinate show people around. The point of this walking the garden, and the walks were often extensive, was centred on the visitor, or to put it another way, those who elected to be engaged in what the landscape garden presented. And this was multiple. From temples to classical allusion, every garden had its vignettes. Just taking the circuitous route, with its sightlines, encouraged contemplation.

William Chambers in the early 18th century was one of the few who had been to China. He loved to introduce the exotics of that land to his landscape gardens. He also liked to juxtapose buildings evocative of other cultures. So Chambers confronted visitors with Moorish constructions and ruined arches and temples to the classical gods. Such gardens had internationalism at their core and invited the unseen to be present. The topiary garden displayed fantastical shapes, but in surrounding, close,

evergreen figures. Theirs was not the vista or the thinking beyond, but wandering close in, not the countryside but the unfamiliar presence nearby. These were not private gardens, but locations to raise vistas in the mind, far beyond restricted thoughts. In time, as mentioned, Chambers' designs became part of the public botanic gardens at Kew.

Each garden has a visual statement to encourage its mood music, now and in the past, but creativity can be invested in both past and present dimensions. One good immediate return is to witness the colour in flowers. They can contrast or meld into each other. Or they can reside next to each other in only one colour as in the white planting, for example, at Sissinghurst Castle. There Vita Sackville-West wanted flowers of one colour. Of course, this was contrasted with the green hedging and the green leaves, but they augmented her core idea. Gertrude Jekyll by contrast constructed her famous herbaceous borders on the principle of colour contrasts.

To get close to anything planted try drawing or painting it. It does not have to become a classical portrait of a botanical specimen, but drawing has the great advantage of making you look more closely. Remembering the plant becomes an absorbing exercise. Trying to find lines and colours for leaves, stems and flowers ingrains the specifics of shading, shape and hue. No matter what the outcome, the memory and the mind are trained. Looking has an effect on the immaterial substance of mind and memory.

The element of time is also crucial. We are very used to gearing up, in sporting events for example, where they compete for ever-faster running or racing times and cars, where they have to impose speed limits; both have become models for how we worship ever-quicker use of time. Plants are slow. They have their own time, subject to conditions of soil, or light or watering. Time is their own or not their own. Sometimes it seems forever until they flower. I go to visit them and see how they are developing,

and they sometimes still remain in their budded shape for longer than I think possible. My amaryllis for Christmas has taken days and weeks to emerge in its dinosaur length and has not yet emerged in its floral charm although I would impatiently say 'time is up'.

Time should slow with the time of plants. Time should count as interactive. It makes room for the impact of other, sometimes elemental, things. We should not begrudge it, taking into account what we dismiss as seasonal, as weather conditions, as the vagaries of sun or rain.

The slowness – or sudden bursts – of growth in plants makes for a different time-keeping that gives hope against the sometimes artificial and mechanical measure we are subject to by strict adherence to programming of all sorts. How can it be wrong to escape the norm of hurry-hurry time and adopt the slow-growth time of plants?

The very idea that time can come in different variations – and can be chosen – brings surprising benefits to the individual. Take, for example, recovering from illness. There is great benefit in watching the slow growth of plants developing. They do not burst out all at once. Rather they grow in tandem with conditions as they perceive them. In a severe winter they halt stems and tender leaves. In mild weather they bring fresh green. It is a matter of perception. It is a matter they take into their own hands, a decision of their own as they look to the benefit in their surroundings. This is nothing at all to do with mathematics in a straight, advancing line.

Maybe the trees we watch have the correct attitude, they grow magnificent in their slow growth. It takes years. Their branching out, and their tree rings, reflect the brightness or lack of goodness the seasons held. Sometimes their erratic arms do not fully reach. But their seeking of the light produces an array of delightful twigs and soft green leaves. What the trees are not are uniform mechanical robots; they have infinite variety and subtlety.

Plants are mirrors of the soul, that all-encompassing representation of the spiritual and the physical. The benefit of all these quiet types is to enhance your life. Even if all that can be managed is a pot-grown, leafy thing, it matters. In a plant you have a companion that might alter your habitual speediness and convert it to a caring, loving, observant slowness.

Garden time becomes a quality that makes human experience matter. We become companioned by nature and more happily live with her.

❧

Paradise – The Ideal Garden

IN THE DARK SPACE where light no longer penetrates all kinds of things are feeling their way, mutating and pushing out shoots. Periodically we need this absence of surface rigmarole. Let the method of how plants grow – indeed their virtual absence – reintroduce the concept, or the contemplation, of life changing, perhaps unseen.

The ideal is paradise, but without detail it is nothing. Plants, flowers, herbs, trees and the vital life-giving element water are part of paradisiacal imagining. Sometimes it is a reality beyond us and we gaze in wonder: we are in paradise. But it is like the rain clouds we need periodically. It passes and comes again and we pray for that revisiting, because we need both water and paradise. We can live and dream in the ideal garden, but we also have to work and exist in the real ones.

In life, paradise is our projection of the garden in complete form, we can savour it. We are not above tasting divine apples. But falling out of paradise, the earth takes us in, we now know what the apple tastes like. Why not think of the apple tree as if it were the tree of life, with roots in the underworld, stem and branches upon this earth and its tiptop growth in the sky, the above full of clouds and the moon and stars? Adam was an innocent, but he had soon to contend with the necessities of life. Paradise became only something he had known in his imagination.

The tree of life is the image we need to see as the tiers we might walk through. In the landscape garden it is often seen as the Greek Elysian Fields, where the yet-living were enabled to speak to the dead to glean advice that aided them. In paintings, many gods are assembled and either nature or the garden extends the often mired-down existence of humankind into the Garden

of Eden. Christianity has a stake in paradise, as does Islam and Judaism, as well as the great Eastern religions

In the landscape garden, paradise is a place in which to wander: a refreshment of inner ideas. This is the extension of the 'garden' – another, but perfected, beautiful place. It presents all walks of life with refuge, with a safe harbour.

All gardens on the plane above the real are at the same time part of the natural garden. It is this interrelationship which is crucial. If explored it goes into mythical stories of gardens in the East, from which spring the very first ideas of verdant, green gardens. Prominent among them is the story of Gilgamesh, the revered and mythical king in Babylonia, who sang the praises of what was Mesopotamia. Flowering plants and many trees for shade grew in the courtyards of the palaces he and others built. The fruits and vegetables grown in these gardens were used in part to make offerings to the gods.

By the first millennium BC, water was channelled through rocks and displayed in gardens. These were the real gardens of the elite. In imperial Nineveh parks and gardens were laid out. Copious fruits, including apples, pears, quinces and almonds, were gathered and the shade of cedar and cypress graced the hot lands. Not least, the Hanging Gardens of Nebuchadnezzar II were legendary and provided a series of verdant terraces. All these Middle Eastern gardens were cultural entities that are no longer extant. But they remain in the mind. They were keenly thought out places where beauty and culture were revered and places of retreat alongside the joys of courtly life.

Arcadia was envisioned by the Greeks, and they loved the 'sacred grove', a place of unspoilt, natural woodland held dear by the gods. Sacred places were cultivated where the flowering plants of the earth were dedicated to particular gods and goddesses. The Golden Apples of the Hesperides is one instance, as are the fabled roses of King Midas. At the earliest temples, the flowerbeds were arranged to complement each stone column.

These special places, *loci amoeni*, were set apart by their unearthly atmosphere from the natural landscape in Greece. Yet there was also continuity, as special places often resided next to agricultural land. They become intertwined as humans reached out to gods and goddesses. Parts of the landscape were planted for utilitarian purpose, but not far from them, and augmenting beauty and pleasure, were the lands of the gods and goddesses. The courtyards may have been under the royal keepers; but the groves were natural and honoured by everyone. There is continuity of cultures here too because whether directly associated or not, trees in groves were sacred to Celtic peoples on the outskirts of Europe as well as the Greeks. They are guarded today as 'ancient' woods. In long tradition and natural heritage, Greeks and Celtic lands intertwine.

In fact, it is of little use to disentangle as solely utilitarian woods which, even today, have the character of mysterious pathways, shaded and endless, if not dark and threatening, from the sacred. It takes little imagining to transport the mind from clobbering the tree in the mindless utility of today to the veneration it held in the past. The woodcutters of the past asked the spirit of the tree if they could wield their axe. The Wild Hunt of folklore certainly swayed rooftops, chimneys and the branches of trees as it rambunctiously gathered hounds and fierce fighters to swoop down from the heavens on the unwary.

Historians are careful to distinguish the origins and then succession of what appeared and when. But all we want to recall is the inception of the garden and the 'sacred grove' as central to creative culture. A special place, such as trees densely growing in a grove, may be designated by humans as a mystical place, harbouring the gods. The site is seen as very beautiful and unique and local people value the trees as divine. The transference of nature into a special arrangement through intervention of human desire and design does not preclude its spontaneously entering another dimension. The sacred wood may have this quality by itself. The garden almost certainly invites its maker or visitor to go beyond what at first seems only planting. Paradise is an envisioned thing: it does not eliminate, it invites thought and entices visitors, especially otherworldly ones, to come and appreciate.

A garden as paradise has healing qualities. They are bequeathed by the centuries, not just the glancing looks we might give them today. They incorporate flowers, shade and water. Hadrian's villa is a case in point. It was visited by classical scholars of every nation because it combined the Roman ideal of garden and villa, one of the greatest legacies we have. The emperor

April
began with rain

Hadrian built his villa at Tivoli. It was opulent and splendid. The combination of intimacy and the dominance of space – its terraces looked extensively over the countryside – fixed for centuries the dual purpose of some European gardens. The managed walks criss-crossed in geometric patterns the wide spaces of the laid-out gardens. At the same time the palace was still at its heart. This founded the long tradition of gardens strategic to the house and the sightlines of the house extending to the garden.

Of course, this reference includes baroque Versailles, the grand palace of the French Sun King, Louis XIV. He possessed the perfect terrain and employed the architect, André Le Nôtre. But in his splendid layout, it is wise to recall his fountains. They are full of frogs and rising gods, who drive chariots out of the glinting waters. And they have carefully contrived – and contained – wilderness. These are part of the carefully laid out paths. The garden is orderly, but it still is mighty in evoking the supernatural.

Gardens aspire to be paradise, elevating the user to rise above the base design and nurturing contemplation by looking beyond the earthly realm. Nature is made into art in a different form.

One of the great influences, despite a significant passage of time is that of Arabic and Islamic concepts of the garden as paradise. In the Koran the paradise reached after death is a garden full of running water, shade and fruit trees. A symbol of life and hope, the garden was part of a consciousness always there in the mind and emotions. It was present as the end of a good life. Arabic culture also introduced water in the form of a fountain which streamed outwards in four quarters.

This form of geometric quartering was, however, more ancient and brought together by many faiths. The Book of Genesis has life-giving water at the centre of the Garden of Eden. It watered the garden and became four riverheads. These patterns are recalled in the Revelation of St John which completes the Christian Bible. In Buddhist iconography this water of life spawns four rivers that symbolise fertility and timelessness. Very ancient is the belief that four is a sacred number which carries with it the fundamental four elements: fire, water, air and earth. Viewed in this context the garden as it developed over the centuries began as one of the most essential tableau accompanying humankind. The garden was an imaginative, desirable entity, even after death; it was the ideal, and also the reality, of green beauty and perfection.

The imaginary garden, as much as the real one, carries us forward. Whatever we make of a green space, there are a great number of gardening ideas that float, much as rain or sunshine does, within our grasp. We make even a small garden in the wake of centuries of symbolic uses of trees, flowers, herbs and fruit. Like food, some of it pleases the palate and some, with its pure scent, sends us messages that the mind ingests.

The divine gift of water was felt most highly in arid countries, but the ancient gardens took hold in Spain in Seville, Cordova and Granada. The Muslim courts and fountains prospered in an architecture of enclosure. The Alhambra is testament to the enduring Moorish quartering of a lion guarded fountain and its meaningful outflow.

But the classical Roman period and the influence of the ancient Middle East met a low point as the last emperor of the Romans was deposed. In 476 AD Charlemagne set declining gardens to rights with his decree that towns should plant gardens with at least 73 herbs and 16 fruit and nut trees. His advisors were in large part the abbots of medieval monasteries, which were now increasing, in numbers, wealth and gardening skills.

But in this history, the spiritual meaning that accompanied the revival of garden lore is often forgotten. Charlemagne presided over great tracts of Europe and was keen to reverse the poverty that had sprung up – a subsistence constrained by primitive methods of cultivation. His drive was to feed and educate through practical learning. This connection to every one of his subjects was at heart religious.

The monasteries took seriously the most vital aspects of gardening. As we have seen, they tended to the ailing and infirm through their care and derived knowledge through Herbals and the remedies cultivated in the gardens and administered in the infirmaries attached to them. They treasured learning and read the Herbals, first in manuscript and after 1470 in print, all that mattered for curing the ill. But above all they valued the symbolic meaning of flowers in the *hortus conclusus* (enclosed garden) which often pictured the Virgin Mary and the Christ Child.

In the walled enclosure many flowers were dedicated to the virtues of Mary. Thus, the heavenly aura came into the garden where such flowers were growing, often as seedlings in the grassy sward that was beloved as a planting medium. But planting herbs as efficacious remedies and cultivating the enclosed garden as a way to heaven, was not the whole picture. The monasteries' heartland was the abbey church in their midst. The whole complex was connected through plants and water flowing throughout. However, it was life dedicated to spiritual goodness that was the underpinning focus of monastic life. Gardens and orchards expressed this in their own unique ways. It was this devotion that Charlemagne wished to spread.

Monasteries had an international view of sharing fruit, vines, flower seeds and Herbals. The abbots and priors came and went between houses dedicated to religion and brought knowledge and the needed plants with them. The secular kings, queens and nobility had the same international reach and were also immersed in the values of gardens. Their practice was to see in these manifestations the value of outward pleasures. They gave priority to their own courting, banquets and private preserves. The *hortus conclusus* became more a garden of delight. It was enclosed by vine trellises, trees for shade, fruit trees for delicacies, flowers as special plants and the green strips of rectangular adornment. These were to the outer eye similar to the places reserved for heavenly contemplation, but they became exclusive domains of pleasure.

Perhaps in the 21st century it is again significant that we integrate the spiritual with all other endeavours, even though the most basic plane of the garden is soil – earth compounded of clay and sand or enriched by organic compost.

Meaning can be extended through trees, flowers and vegetables. How they are ordered is emotional and reasoned perception. Take two historic possibilities: the baroque love of surprise and wonder, its grottoes and outstanding excesses and see them alongside the geometry and garden statues of the Renaissance palace. Each is ordered in a different way, but each reaches out to mythical beings. The garden is not just geometry that by its avenue leads to a noble house, or the circuitous route that hides and then reveals a Palladian mansion. It is what the garden and its wandering provoke. It can be the elusive presence of the god Pan or it can reach towards heaven in Paradise.

One grand idea is to think of gardens of the past as rich enclaves out of time. Labyrinths and mazes were favourites in centuries past, and they remain so now. Their intricacies served many purposes. A Celtic one was to trace this pattern of labyrinth to invoke the otherworld, so that divining the future became possible. Another was within a cathedral. There it represented a pilgrimage, usually to Jerusalem, for the person who could not go to the city itself. The footsteps, or proceeding on knees, followed the convolutions in a tight space on the cathedral floor and meant travel to Jerusalem as a heavenly city, not a place on earth. Those who could travel there were also not primarily interested in its physicality. The point was to commune in paradise and in supplication. On the island Of Iona far to the west of Scotland, Abbot Adomnan dreamed and wrote about the holy places of the East.

Labyrinths and mazes were real in gardens. Here they were constructed of hedges, perhaps box, yew or evergreens of another sort. To be lost in paths with dead ends or be bemused as to the way out could be taken as a metaphor of life. But it was also the kind of game indulged in for pleasure in a garden. These labyrinths were often constructed in Renaissance gardens because of their obsession with perspective and geometry. The engagement in circular paths, invisible from outside or in, with their thick hedges, were favourites for lovers or trysts of every kind. These labyrinths had mystical meaning, but they also had secular uses. Today they are in fashion again. They represent getting lost in every way and then finding liberation as the sudden turn of freedom is disclosed to brings him or her to face the world again.

Most garden books make paradise sound as if it had taken

its place on earth. But quite the reverse is true. Gardens, be they ornate or the preserve of needed vegetables, point the other way. Sitting in the fashioned garden, even looking from it to the undulating wild hills, or walking the grounds with its many variations, the outside is taken inwards or, in an opposite direction : we are enabled to encompass lands imagined or dreamed. Never has that ability to rediscover paradise been so important in human life. And gardens are ready to play a central role, as they always have done since human culture began.

Secret Gardens

OUR GARDEN IS NOT just what we assemble to grow up from the ground. As we have seen, it comes rooted in centuries of layouts with their design intentions and specific meanings. In recalling the past, we transport ourselves into future possibilities: imagining is an essential component. And some of the richest imaginings have come from folklore and children's books. In these narratives we are not restricted to the supposedly 'real'. If we are honest, our mind and its 'eye' has much more to contemplate than bare facts. We sense unseen presences and perceive things beyond the merely visible.

This is apparent, for example, in gardens which are read about in literature. In the classics of up to 100 years ago, authors explored 'time out of time' dilemmas of choosing who you are. Time and its numerical progression are sometimes subverted in these stories. This is to the advantage of the garden as a place of meditation which can be beyond time.

In the books discussed here, gardens are a liberating place, because they do not follow convention, introducing, for example, ghosts of lives past which are viable and even talkative. But beyond that they are a place of redemption. Their seasonal rotation gives the hope of change, and this is realised not only in the garden, but by the characters, who are on the verge of adulthood. On the other hand, a suspension of time allows for the realisation of potential and clarity in who we are becoming – and would like to be. This is not just true for children; it remains valid for all ages and conditions. Suspended time is a necessity for all by generating the creativity that is essential to life, no matter what we do.

The garden in all these vital fictions is the place where forces gather and the selection begins. The reflection on different kinds of experience is rooted in the surroundings. The garden, and the landscape it is in, provide necessary escape from the hustle bustle of everything else. The surroundings of greenery and its regeneration, not once but in every season, year upon year, change our outlook. It has a different progression and thus invigorates change when we ourselves are ready to grow.

The Secret Garden, by Frances Hodgson Burnett, a Victorian writer, touches on a quality we can deem timeless and useful for the present. Her setting is not something familiar to us as she begins the story. It is a castle in Yorkshire with many mysterious rooms. The heroine, Mary Lennox, is a child on the verge of becoming grown-up, bereaved by the loss of her parents. She is sent, as an ugly orphan, to be under the charge of a distant and absent guardian.

This very forlorn situation, almost hopeless, begins a story of redemption, both for her and other children on the cusp of growing up. One of them, Colin, is seriously disabled. Mary Lennox slowly learns independence. She is unused to dressing herself, for example. She was in command of servants in India but because they determined so much, she was very restricted in her actions. This does not work in her new surroundings and she listens, at first unwillingly, to the maid in charge of her. She learns to dress herself. Her curiosity awakens and she begins to understand both herself and how she is connected to others and to nature beyond. She changes and explores; then explores and changes.

The first thing she discovers is a cranky yet dedicated gardener, whose friend is the robin redbreast who comes to sit on his spade. This garden bird is the first friend who leads Mary to a secret garden. She discovers a door hidden in the ivy. This opens on to the garden where the robin nests and where she suddenly discovers bulbous life, edging into springtime green and springtime

flowering. For the very first time she kneels on the ground and
grubs in the soil to aid these signs of the goodness to come. They,
and the wild roses, which must be checked and trained to bloom
their best, reveal to her the power of something not under her
control, but nonetheless indigenous to her, expanding in bounty
and meaningfulness. She has found the loveliness that waits for
no man and each season begins its cycle of renewal and growth.

   This story has inherent magic, often said to work as a blessing, since the children become healthier and more enamoured of their future. They start doing things on their own initiative. Mary, wandering through the hidden and locked parts of the castle finds Colin, the abandoned child of her guardian. The guardian is grown up, but crippled and despairing. He is hardly ever there. To Colin she says, forthrightly, unlike the accommodating adults, that lying in bed is silly. This is wording that all the servants and the doctor have shied away from uttering. Mary is direct. She will show Colin how to get out of bed and show him the secret garden.

She finds more friends, step by step, and shares them with the self-centred Colin. Dickon, her mentor, is the other central character in the story. He is the same age as she, perhaps slightly older. Dickon knows the creatures of the Yorkshire moorland and they trust and love him. He is always surrounded by squirrels, rabbits, foxes and other animals. He is integrated in a way she is not. But he helps her in finding what is essential. And, eventually, Colin benefits from knowing him as well. It is Dickon, along with Mary, who helps Colin overcome himself. He teaches Colin to walk by himself, which is a breakthrough moment for body and soul.

The garden is the crux of all the children's lives. They see its renewal and growth. Each participates in the natural wonder of resuscitated lives. The ugly Mary becomes more expressive, more sure of herself. Colin learns to walk by himself, no longer insistent he will surely die if the grown-ups do not accede to his every wish. Dickon will be forever faithful to the animals and plants of his beloved moors, but he has gained human company now as well.

This is a story of seasons, and spring is what makes for all growth. Girl and boy discover this truth and start to live it through their own experience. This participation is the essence of the narrative. Imagine how bare the world would be, if that groundwork of spring and the awakening seasons came ignored and empty handed. It takes a children's story to loosen the sorry bonds of adult intoxication with sophisticated things which obscure the essence of humanity. A place like the secret garden illuminates that not-so-secret, elemental region that leads to change and healing.

The secret garden is a place not easily dismissed. It expands above all in the mind. Burnett's tale has become classic because it implies that there is a hard to define, shadowy, maybe sunlit, garden in the imagination and emotions that awaits discovery. It suggests that we experience the validity of nature, no matter who or where we are.

Lucy M Boston, writing late in life, says that true revelation of growing up came for her when she explored the smell, colour and mystery of the Kent River estuary. She has nothing good to say about her upbringing, making it almost monstrous in the description she gives, but then she suddenly her heart waxes lyrical when she comes upon landscape and the gardens of nature, both ordered and wild:

> Now in Arnside I received the full impact of the returning sun. Every inch of that earth responded. There were fields of wild daffodils, those slender little plants with white haloes and primrose trumpets, infinitely more beautiful than the dandelion coloured giants of today... In the open country and across the commons the primroses and violets were everywhere while the smell of the earth itself was intoxicating. The scent of a bunch of primroses must be one of the sweetest things in childhood...
>
> Beyond the farm was a hill covered with limestone, at the summit of which were the Fairy Steps, the object of our excursions. We went through a wood where the trees grew out of crevices between horizontal limestone strata. The crevices were full of ferns and mosses and of un-guessed depth, very mysterious. The stone was a pale bluish-silver, half-polished, which gave a curious light to the wood. The

Fairy Steps, small, regular and absolutely natural, wound up through a crack just wide enough for children to pass, almost impossible for buxom Nurse, on to a plateau. This was before the era of trippers and there was nothing to diminish the magic.[1]

Lucy Boston's stories are extensions of her own best times. She elaborates on her house, a very old one in the Fens, and inhabits it with children that follow their imagination. But a very large part of this is the sounds and smells of the fenlands and the magic of its rivers. In the stories this is often the unnamed River Ouse. The children she invents become Boston's explorers. She recounts their daily discoveries as they let birds into their rooms or wander the sometimes enigmatic, sometimes frightening, now and again welcoming, garden around the manor house of Green Knowe. They even encounter ghost children in the garden. It is an intricate otherworld, but productive in that the imagination is not curbed. It follows its own rules yet connects with a life to which we can all have access.

The same is true, for example, in gliding down the waters and discovering the river. As the story progresses the children encounter ever more strange-seeming appearances looming at them in the by-ways and watery keeps the children find using their canoe. There are eccentric men, winged and fleeting horses, giants that wind up in the circus, but who resemble, at first, uprooted tree trunks. In stark contrast, there is the restricting world of adults, who see the rules, but not the fanciful creatures.

This approach chides those of us who think they have left childhood behind. There is a world to explore, making believe beyond, and free of our rational curtailments. This world of gardens is more than the stalk in front of us. The story waiting to be told from inside us is more than the facts we accumulate. It is worth breathing in and out deeply, liberating the glory as well

---

[1] Lucy M Boston, *Memories*, p.58–60

as the angst inside. Children's literature is worth the emulation it rarely receives.

The imagination that Lucy Boston lets loose can cause disbelief, but it carries the niggling, happy thought that deep within we are ready to concur. The imaginative side lurks in all people, young, old and disabled. To call it forth is another healing aspect. Because without wanting to go beyond it, the present can never be realised. The power of the imagination comes from our many unfathomable experiences, including childhood. If the imagination of when we were young is crippled to admit only the staid and reasonable, we are diminished. Be it as fertile as it can be and we rise above the mundane to become absorbed into the rich possibility of what may be, what can be. In this way we see potential rather than restriction in our gardens of existence. Everyone needs to go beyond the present, perhaps especially those hampered by physical limitations.

Often nature and the imagined are at the root of the story. In BB's *The Little Grey Men*, the fantasy writer Dennis Watkins-Pitchford recounts the adventures of gnomes The line between his natural river with the animals that call its banks home, the beginning of spring and its waiting fertility, is blurred with the folkloric. What is deemed reality is then called into question because the life of the gnomes blends so well into the description of the natural world.

The story begins with the hopefulness that always accompanies spring. In this it reflects the realisation that *The Secret Garden* has engendered: even the deprived learn to walk upright in the discovery that there are others willing to share; there are others willing to brave an enclosed garden. Or is it the sharing and growing that makes hope valuable?

Adventures start in the light of spring. This is the author setting the scene for the ups and downs of going forth on a quest for the missing gnome:

> It was one of those days at the tail end of winter when spring, in some subtle way, announced its presence. The hedges were still purple and bristly, the fields bleached and bitten, full of quarrelling starling flocks; but there was no doubt about it, the winter was virtually done with for another seven months. The great tide was on the turn, to creep so slowly at first, and then to rise ever higher to culminate in the glorious flood, the top of the tide, at midsummer.
>
> Think of it! All the power, all those millions of leaves, those extra inches to be added to bushes, leaves and flowers. It was all there under the earth, though you would never have guessed it.[2]

The secret garden is both subtle and obvious. It reaches another dimension in *Tom's Midnight Garden* written by Philippa Pearce. Here, in another time than the present, the Victorian, Tom crosses over through the chiming of an old grandfather clock in the night, hours from a modern, subdivided former mansion. He is both ghost and real. His attachment to the girl, Hattie, becomes evident as a growing boy to a girl who is sometimes younger, sometimes more mature. All is dependent on his time-travel. In the end he meets the real Hattie, an old woman. This is the woman, who, when she was young, saw Tom as anything but

---

[2] BB, *The Little Grey Men*, Introduction, p.1

a ghost in the surroundings of the garden that was as seemingly unreal as time-travel. Her testimony corroborates his adventures as true.

Again, with this story, the imagined becomes real. What is important here is the interplay. The past does not inevitable materialise as the present. It is always night-time when Tom engages his adventures. The Selves that the story of Tom reveals evolve as a part of the night side of everyone. It is a continuum, yet mysterious and to be entered as a dimension of the Self unknown to our safer, more mundane, daylight hours. The adults in the story are removed, reasonable, even loving, but they have no inkling of night-time delving. But this is vital to true knowing, although it manifests only gradually, an unveiled facet, this secret tasting of a past which is also present.

Tom enters a garden non-existent in the present time in the middle of the night when he manages to unlock a door that normally leads to garages and bins. He experiences this garden in its intimacy, its weathers, its seasons, its layout. He gets to know the orphan Hattie, a young girl, then in random sequence as more grown-up. She wears Victorian clothes and has the habits of her time; nevertheless she is as adventuresome as he. And she sees Tom, both for what he is, as well as through his appearing to her as a ghost. The past is not seen as progressive, in accord with the time sequence to which we are accustomed: appearing now in winter, now in summer, now with older boys present, now with Hattie maturing. The adventures of the night are always a surprise. They can materialise in any time since they are not dependant on the clock – the grandfather clock does not register this time of imaginative escape on its minute face.

Time is suspended, and this is important for the development of what Tom can perceive, and what we can all perceive. In these adventures the formation of personality comes with the starts and stops of perception, of learning who you are or might be. Never is this a function of counting minutes in the units of clock-time.

The garden in *Tom's Midnight Garden* seems to enlarge, widen out. In a zigzag wandering sort of way, it is explored, but all of this depends on the increasing involvement of Tom with Hattie. Then, towards the end of the book, both become enamoured of skating on the river's ice. It is Tom who tries out the Victorian skates, but both set off on the frozen river that runs through the Fens, the Ouse. Suddenly the garden is left behind, and in the glitter of winter, the two let breezes and swiftness guide their lives. They are running and skating into the bigness of country, with no confines. This liberation ends the story. It leads us to meditating on the possibility that we may be travelling in dimensions that are bigger than we think. We may add our own alternatives as we 'skate' the world.

These wider worlds can be dark like the midnight garden and may envelop us all. But they are not theoretical like Sigmund Freud's Oedipal complexes and unconscious subjections to mother or father figures. They give space to the widening Self that may lurk or lie hidden through those unbidden, quiet corners of the soul. The beauty of the story remains in the unstated meaning of what is only revealed in the narrative, and what we absorb from its telling and retelling. No matter what precise lesson may be drawn from a midnight garden that is not really there, the Self is encouraged to open those doors.

Children's books and tales are enchanting because they stimulate personal dynamics. Who is it that says an end is reached when we reach the grown-up stage? Tom's exasperating guardian, his uncle, makes us think about all having a concise and explained background. But we come to know better. At the end of the story Tom's essential meeting with the old Hattie, who Tom now realises owns the house that has been turned into flats, and preserves the grandfather clock, proves in our 'real' time that none of this was a figment of Tom's imagination. The garden was a real garden, which cultivated the dark, and then illumined the corners – and walls – it contained. *Tom's Midnight Garden* is a lesson, but not a didactic lesson by any means. It remains a children's story that we should be encouraged to read, about a garden that we can all discover, if we are brave and child-like enough.

A Traveller in Time by Alison Uttley enjoys similar classic status. Again, the author is harking back to pleasures of the countryside she once knew. They are dear to her and she opens for us the memory of beloved but lost intimacy. The smells and lighting of kitchen fires; the furniture polished and maintained, though age old; the competence of the housewife and the liveliness of servants of every order – all these things are beautifully evoked and make her childhood ours. The world has not ceased to change, but the look back is enchanting. This magic enables the reader yet again to go through doors into a time that is remote yet near. The garden is here, the countryside, but its meadows, woods and fields are close and described so lovingly that we know them as if we were Penelope the child heroine. Suddenly we walk them, with her, and we see them with her eyes.

The story is about travelling, but not as we know it from geography. Places are exchanged, but while resembling each other visually they are altered in time. The impact lies in the mind's eye. Penelope travels back and forth to the time of Mary Queen of Scots as this noble lady is held prisoner. But not even she knows when these time shifts will occur. The Babington plot attempts to rescue Mary, but it is doomed. Penelope has hindsight – but she cannot express it, or only in part, as she is introduced to the household in these former times. She comes to love this time travel as much as she loves her aunt and uncle in whose venerable home she has come in her present life to reside for a holiday.

Her usefulness in the past to which she is transported, as well as her love for Thackers, the old farm where she is happily integrated, make it very obvious how she thrives in this connecting landscape of meadows, brooks, fields and kitchen gardens. She is at home here, as the author was at Castle Top, the farm of her

childhood. Alison Uttley pays eloquent tribute to a landscape, now gone, that perpetuated the old ways. She revives them in the imagination, relating their goodness, while never grumbling how arduous it the older way of life must have been.

Being transported like this is valid for us all regardless of age. In her children's book, Uttley has no inhibition in presenting a golden age, and we concur. She enables us to look at what is no longer present but can be brought happily to life. We tend to dismiss that kind of evocation as nostalgic, because it is not fraught with cares and woes. We seem uneasy without the unhappiness that may arise for us so frequently. But what exactly is wrong with projecting a 'golden age'? Would it not be more sanguine to include 'golden ages' in our thoughts and emotions?

Alison Uttley entwines her retrospective love of early childhood with wonders. Then she could entertain the trees, young
animals, herbs, hedges and many other things as living, even talking. These become moments in 'time out of time'. Uttley enables
us to read her encounters with nature and to visualise what she
sees. Thus her 'now' becomes a minute within our own time. And
by that means, we learn to appreciate a utopia. In reading books
meant for children we dive towards our own wants. It should be
a necessity that we are guided, encouraged to picture what shines
as delight in our own eyes.

In creating two worlds, Alison Uttley lets us be free of one
or the other. None of us is bound to either. We are free to move.
Lucy Boston was just as adamant in her *Memories* that cars were
an afterthought and she much preferred horse-drawn carriages.
She writes:

> If I were quick enough off the mark, I usually got a seat on
> the box next to the driver where besides being high above
> the hedges with a good view of the country, I could enjoy the
> rolling rumps of the horses, and the piston-like movement of
> their stifles, together with the rich smell of horse and leather,
> the jingle, the tossing and the musical clip-clop.[3]

These authors of classical children's books make us live in
worlds that are filled with imagination, often located in the past
– sometimes a very real past, sometimes a past only conceivable
in the mind. Nonetheless, to enter worlds created by a perceptive
mind is to experience a rich otherness. In this way join the creative enterprise at some level, whether we edge just past the mundane, or a take a deep and subversive plunge into the fanciful.

What I am pleading for is not to be stuck only in one dimension. The garden and the experience of time-travel it offers stirs
up everything static in our mindset. Exploration happens in

---

[3] Lucy M Boston, *Memories*, p.69

the mind. The physical may be left behind. But it is important to move, even when daydreaming, with creative consistency and awareness. Such daydreaming is not an escape but an adventure in authenticity.

Storytelling is in truth the opposite of escapism, both as an education in what tradition has to offer and as a means of reaching for ourselves the wisdom that folklore and literature have saved over the centuries. It has the great advantage of offering learning without arid theory, letting the listener or reader decide what is meant by its symbolic character. The advantage comes in the detailed elaboration, the use of objects and concrete sensations, to tell of personal things, from irritation to joy.

From imaginary worlds created by children's literature, to storytelling involving age-old creatures, this depth or resonance is the most valuable narrative level for all individuals. It loosens bonds and it enables distancing and insight, both of which are crucial to enrich our understanding and our sense of significance. Much like the discovery of secret gardens within.

But the garden itself has 'voices' that add to where the gaze takes you. The leaves breathe and return you to musings that unite many things, past, present and the city and surrounding countryside. Going into the past may raise the future. Lucy Boston reminds us of the values of reflecting on experiences no longer ours:

> What I want to evoke is the feeling I had at the time, not foreseeing the future, that the past of the house from the beginning still existed – the winds coming off its hay-fields, the clouds trailing shadows across the familiar woods, all the sounds of the familiar song birds, cocks, cattle and sheep, pump and bucket, axe and saw, the overriding tyranny of the seasons, the human fears and isolation, the deep passions and strong earthly loyalties. There was reverence for memory, and the expectation, the belief in a future... I began to make a garden.

Boston reminds us how important each place is and how it has its own specific history and special presence. Making a garden is not just digging up the soil. Gardens connect pasts we barely know with futures we cannot discern. But we can imagine. Boston herself recreated the past centuries of the Norman house which she renovated and which provides the basis of her books. She made the house, Hemingford Grey, known to readers of her children's books as Green Knowe, while physically restoring the house to its earliest origins. It became a combination of the inscrutably old, down even to its ghosts, with her personal tastes.

The authors we have discussed represent only a small selection of literary artists for whom gardens are as rich in metaphor and symbolism as they are in plants. They demonstrate how the garden seems to cross barriers of age, gender, culture and time to provide a near universal language for our human condition. Here again we find spaces, inner and outer, in which we can live, reflect and grow. We can reflect on change at a comfortable pace.

᷍

Art in the Garden

THE LAYOUT OF gardens, as we have explored, is in itself a form of art. But there are other ways that art exerts its influence apart from the arrangement of trees, water and flowers. Perhaps gardens are the most important place where art and nature interact, in a way that both defines and enlarges human potential.

Botanical art is the first and most luxurious form of depicting exactly what vegetation and flowers look like. It has been practised over the centuries and holds fast the detail that all gardeners and those interested in the specifics of plants hold dear. As it was practised by accomplished artists, this form of retaining vital information, like the seeds and leaf structure of flowering plants, became in itself an art form. Books were centred on colour plates and these were reproduced as authoritative sources – at least that was one important reason they were commissioned. They were to be seen as references to be consulted.

Yet botanical illustrations became so much more than reference points, because of their beauty. Each rose, lily, hellebore, even each cabbage was given their graphic and artistic best in the plant's colour-exact depiction. Before mass production, an artist hand-coloured the final plates chosen. The books of botanical art are worth investigation in their own right. They arrest each flower and its specialties on the page. They provide a permanent picture to consult. And, they present scientific exactitude together with the painting's beauty especially when recording plants, often exotics. In the 17th and 18th centuries the drawings and paintings showed plants not yet seen growing in gardens at home, but they accomplished their mission by disseminating knowledge from voyages to distant lands.

Botanical art is particular and difficult to practise. The colours and the forms specific to each and every plant are to be recorded. But these can be added to the healing garden when looking and recognising details is the objective – deeper knowledge and great patience is always the outcome! Often this is more plant-centred than human-centred. As plants are specifically identified around the globe, they are reproduced in various media, among them most recently in photographs. Yet there is something fixed and static in this kind of visual recording.

In nature each plant changes in structure and the way it looks varies with different stages of the year. The colour of leaves alters and the budding and flowering reach their height in sunlit seasons. The vegetation has so many variants according to growth zones and seasons, an encyclopaedic book would be needed to catalogue the specification of each plant, where it lives and what its characteristics are. Through the ages botanical art books have accomplished much, while proving how delightful it is to look at illustrations and learn from them. They have chronicled plants, and some are truly works of art, from the past as well as today's endeavours.

However, the living forms of plants stretches our perceptions and imagination further. Botanical art is easily traced and the books are reproduced widely, and copiously commented upon and summarised. Instead, let us take up other forms of art where the concentration is on interaction between the subject and the everyday observer.

It is important to note the range from exactness in botanical art, where the attributes of the plant is precisely reproduced, to the plant in suggestive forms, such as unruly grasses that are hinted at or only used in abstraction. Maybe the grasses are there to give colour in a painting that makes trees only daubs while the water reflections given are only a zigzag to suggest light. The snaking, quivering, darker, watery tones may then be the more exciting ones. Even if the trees are only blotches, the grasses only an indication and the sky is blotted out with tissue to show

clouds, it is nature in this abstraction that is intensely observed. Maybe the work has its genius, just in this play of forms.

When Claude Monet lost his sharper eyesight, he painted the light on water lilies. Their more abstract form, which he experimented upon in his late paintings, lent itself to his new creation. He was observing; he was painting. In truth he was evoking new kinds of looking and today we take pleasure in his way of seeing. We can now perceive what he saw. Monet saw colour, saw light, saw reflection, saw the darker waters.

Was Monet moving ahead of nature or discovering something in nature that was as yet unperceived? Or both together. This closer union between what is seen by the artist and the momentary manifestation of plant or flower life is the focus here. Again, this is fragmentary but vital: how plants are seen, integrated, telescoped, diminished, enhanced, portrayed in whatever stage plants are in and trying to evolve them in different forms, to put them in a different medium. Just as a diverting thought – plants reveal themselves even in a documentary form as dried specimens on paper, such as in an herbarium. Yet they remain outcrops from one organic root.

In these myriad forms what is important is the action. Every painting in whatever medium means close scrutiny and an involvement in looking. Decisions have to be made about shape, scale and approach. My preferred medium is watercolour. It is in one sense unpredictable. The colours spread of their own accord, and one has to work from light to dark, overlaying it with other colours or not, or working wet-on-wet or wet-into-dry and so on. Again there are numerous books on watercolour techniques. But it is essential that you look intensely and judge what is entering your picture. This close attention in a living moment on subjects that vary with the season and that you are catching for that moment in time gives us that crucial connection with nature. It binds each person that attempts this more lovingly or frustratingly to the plant, the garden, the scene, the countryside.

Beyond the close view is that of the landscape. This is positioning of a different sort. No single thing, for example a still life of flowers in a vase, dominates, but this and that element, distant and close in their right perspective, is selected. The view, what is to be excluded, how clouds form, how water reflects the sky, the mood, the whole composition matters. This opens the view in a landscape garden to new scrutiny. What is more, many of the views were constructed and these paintings record what the designer shaped. Through the painting the mood, for example in a graphic, bucolic, lawn-and-sheep approach, precludes what could otherwise be recorded as more dramatic. A topographic representation is calmer than a stormier one! A Claude Lorrain could be pitched against a Salvator Rosa. Both were Baroque artists and knew each other. Claude Lorrain depicted the then new art of landscape painting. It was calm and gave life to beautiful trees and clouds and vistas. Salvator Rosa chose more striking landscapes with storms and lightening to enhance dramatic encounters.

But let us proceed onward from work on canvas and other blank sheets, remembering the observation and planning that these require. Let us return to gardens and a form which has progressed as gardens have taken their different shapes, augmenting their structure. What was always integrated in the garden – and what we take note of as defining presences – are the sculptures.

Sculpture has adorned gardens since time immemorial. In nooks and crannies, in the open, or around a bend, when you come upon it, all planting is raised to a new significance by a carefully chosen and well positioned object. The big landscape gardens made reference to myths, for example, and raised temples to house the gods. The landowners and designers (not always the same) saw this as a path to enhancing nature, by gathering cultural meanings that gardens in themselves sometimes lacked. In the addition of a sculpture or statue, or an ornamental building among flowers or trees, the garden achieved significance and added a dimension of contemplation and feeling. Such encounters with statuary and temples offered the visitor new visions, as if waking simultaneously in another plane.

What sculpture has to offer in a world dominated by nature is a startling, sudden insight into the significance of the visual encounter. What is seen is no longer neutral or ambiguous, yet can point to what may confront, or be revealed, right beside us, as of pressing significance. How this is achieved is guided by design and the making of the artwork. The garden creator wishes to lead the onlooker straight to the meaning the sculpture represents. And the onlooker adds his or her own vision to that message. Gardens that lack such encounters miss out on a dimension beyond what the landscape can supply.

A contemporary garden, in contrast to one of the historic

styles of centuries ago, enhances the intricacies involved by becoming aware of planting and sculpture, including the carving of
words as indications of what to contemplate. There is no return
to a naïve vision of nature alone. In a well-known Scottish garden, Ian Finlay's Little Sparta, multiple indications of where you
are and the history that has defined the modern world come to
meet you. High in the hills, enduring in what is not lush countryside, Little Sparta is an experience of walking through time. It
is like opening a door and encountering rooms shaped by nature
with words carved in stone or wood or metal that further enhance our thoughts about the past. It brings the modern and past
worlds closer in a decidedly contemporary way.

Sculpture like this is not a long static lesson but an indication. The glancing light enhances the stone, and the words, and
then it includes wayward and wonderfully leafy vegetation. The

two make a difference: the writing never to be erased and the vegetation a varied seasonal augmentation. As visitors we become the third side of the triangle. We acknowledge with this kind of garden the human action of past events and the non-human power of nature. The plant itself merges with the message, in this case an opposite, like stone or metal; the greenly verdant accentuating the hard permanence of words or statues. Whatever the ornament, this confrontation with the cyclical resurgence of plants unites in the mind's eye. There are really three dimensions at work – the signpost for history, the view and the planting. But most intriguing is the spirit of knowing or learning on the part of the visitor. Sculpture provides the necessary 'genius of place' to this garden. The artist and the designer are one and the same.

Feeling is important too, and best when channelled by restrained or mute indications. The hardy 'spartan' mode of Ian Finlay's garden deliberately demonstrates this character. The path and stopping points enhance every view and thus every feeling. Gardens are constructed for consciously experiencing feeling. But well-designed gardens do this by also connecting the mind to emotion. Gardens add sculpture in order to clarify this process and to give contemplation the time and place it deserves.

Little Sparta also allows most of the vegetation to be on the wild side. And many of the plants are natives of Scotland like the birches. This garden is never far removed from a natural resource. What makes it unique is the combination of many moments, often historical, which are tied together in its spaces. These spaces are like rooms that progressively make up a whole human habitation, but in the house of nature. Moment after moment consciousness takes a new turn in what is presented as one continuum. But the indications are often – and consciously – only a fragmentary allusion to history. The garden pathway takes many forms of brick and stone, laid out appropriately. No one takes steps on a path of sameness. The episodes are marked. However, their fragmentary character leaves open the thoughts which may be raised by each.

Sculpture and garden are food for reflection. A garden empty of writing on stone, cryptic and beautiful as it may be, is just a series of plants. Although these may be interesting by themselves, the point made here, in Ian Finlay's garden, is that the varied green shade has an explicit purpose. His garden shows that plants and sculpture belong together. There is contemplation in an object – he does like stones and beautiful lettering – that is set among streams or meadows or trees. These are planted and revelatory to the mind. They may introduce the train of thought intended, but also much more. There is always intention in cryptic wording, such as the clipped and evocative verses of poetry the artist has chiselled throughout.

Little Sparta begins where all European gardens begin, with allusion to Roman times. But the room in the garden devoted to Rome does not begin with a re-creation. Instead there are chopped-off columns which act as reminders but do not let anyone fully enter Rome. So this is not a re-creation but something to ponder. It does not want Rome to be the ideal, especially not what was evoked through neoclassicism – the republican Rome depicted through scenes in landscape gardens. What Finlay wants is more like the ruin we are left with. The past is to be with us and what we have left behind, not least the republican values we have aspired to and which are present in Roman ideals, but which often fail. In other words, the garden makes the wanderer think of these ideals and what might be their value and what we have lost.

To add a further dimension, there are sculptures by others, not chiselled by Ian Finlay and not made in his garden They are embedded additions that take one beyond seasonal plants, which are apt in their own right. I am thinking of a silver wolf, sitting, head bent and lolling tongue, that intrigued me. He was sitting alone under trees in a garden and you come upon his shiny steel brightness all of a sudden. It meant several things to me straight off. Into my mind came the many stories of the wolves such as

Romulus and Remus, and in children's books, the Red Riding Hood stories and its many modern variations, and the howling wolf now restricted when living in the wild, yet creeping back across Europe.

I put the verdant spring plants and blossom together with the unexpected hardness of steel and its shiny presence. The garden became a meditation as well as an investigation of how the plants were grouped, what grew here, and so forth. I had to incorporate the wolf with my pleasant thoughts about myself and what I wanted in my garden.

Again, in the same garden, in shiny steel, a fish on a bicycle confronted me. It was a little bigger than I was and very shiny, situated opposite me on the verge of a pond. This is a modern symbol for women needing men like a fish needs a bicycle and here it was in a garden, quite unexpected.

There were other sculptures, but these two have remained with me. I carried them in my thoughts as much as the glorious, many-blossomed azaleas and magnolias of that spring. This was when I began to think about augmentation; the suddenness of surprise and the opening out of thought that the pathways of nature can evoke. The same experience came to me in the same garden that brought sculpture together with planting. I saw more much than the grouping of plants.

Little Sparta in the Scottish landscape incorporates this provocation by combining man-made signs with nature and its abundance from spring into autumn. Moving from thought and its implanted nature the garden opens from encounter to encounter, room after room. But none of them begin without reflection on human identity and history. No one can lose his or her sense of self in the garden. Nature is cyclical and can be unnerving and brutal, but humankind cannot disentangle itself from nature any more than it can from history – past, present and future. The garden does not separate but envisions an enduring, inescapable partnership. We can be an enhancement to nature, yet we are always learning.

So sculpture in a garden deepens the experience and broadens its frame of reference. Nothing in a garden is meant to be bland. The landscape garden placed gods on earth through statuary and temples; the gardens of the Renaissance did the same, but the different view in their parterres exhibited gods as statuary, in support of myths, that exemplified attributes of the god needed by humans. Each such section provided meditation – and sometimes belief in divine intervention. The Picturesque in later landscape gardens, made emotions and thought a part of every garden. Together with what nature produces, rain or sunshine, squalls, clouds, or storms, the feelings that go with nature accompanied what is seen.

There is a long tradition of the garden providing interactions with supernatural entities – the embodied powers of nature. Think of the many times a visitor confronts Neptune or Triton in gardens, in their caves or lakes, not as in the ocean itself or on a sea-faring vessel. Little Sparta, too, as a garden, invokes the sea. But engraved signs and wind-swept grasses rather than vast stretches of the sea provide this vision. The sea is far away on the coast of Scotland and only touches you through the sounds or movements it makes rather than unending blue from a beach. Grasses, rushes, grain fields, wind in the trees are present, but not the water's waves. They are bound together by Finlay's engraved words and hints that here, too, might lurk the sea, tragedy of a ship's sinking, war and the conflict of the elements. The signs in cryptic, but beautifully incised, writing are invocations. They do not spell out a set interpretation but instead invite rumination. Sombre memories given through the rising waves, or their troughs, is part of what you experience in participating in this garden, even though the sea is distant.

We are often surprised by these connections, finding things side by side in unusual proximity. It is a garden-maker's way to tell a story, but the story charts further voyages through the added imagination of the visitor. Imagination remains essential

to the readings within Ian Finlay's garden. Whether stretching to classical times, calling on Apollo, or memorialising ships sunk in WWI or WWII, eyes are opened by the very terseness of the messages. It is all there, but the allusions depend on our engendered emotions to fully interpret and fulfil the meaning. The modern garden at Little Sparta is unique in its time-travel. It evokes elements and marks the most imaginative interplays with the past. Rome, as well as the French Revolution, is part of its visual play within the stark but rewarding environment of a Scottish hillscape.

This is very different to the sundial, for example, in parterres. There the sundial was an interpreter that brought sun and shadow to people wishing to know the time and other planetary and celestial happenings. It was an artefact at best inducing wonder at these events. The setting in the garden promoted awareness of the influence of the sun on mortals and the growth of plants. It was not there to promote the sense of history, but of more precise time keeping, which was still considered a wonder of the universe.

Little Sparta is a modern garden given to invocations of our history and its entwining with nature. Apollo, who we meet in so many gardens, is evident here as well. He is represented by a figure cut out of red metal, very dynamic and active as he chases Daphne. She evades him and she escapes by turning into a tree. She has called upon her father, the river god Peneus, who has helped her change into a laurel. She is a figure of green metal and her effigy, tousled and fleeing and beautiful, suggests her fate. Apollo adopts the laurel in her honour as his emblem. The garden hints at the turmoil of love.

Of course, Apollo has many other attributes and Finlay's Little Sparta incorporates many of them. The musing on these fateful lovers in this instance gives visitors yet another chance to appreciate the god of art and nature – what others have called nature into art. There is good reason for this – as artificial planting, hybridising and importing plants and flowers have done their fair share in changing gardens. But in this example Apollo's pursuit of the fair nymph Daphne has in Little Sparta taken place in a cultivated, but essentially wild range of trees and plants native to Scotland. It has therefore shown that, in the modern wild garden, gods and nymphs can inhabit a place of wilderness.

Take, as another example of artwork in the garden, the construction of a Chinese temple and look-out in the Royal Botanic Garden Edinburgh. Eloquently silent, it allows the visitor to realise how much the plants around them are imports brought to fruition by their cultivation in this location. The exotic specimens themselves – and the nowadays familiar ones – recall in this setting the efforts of the explorers and the Botanic Garden itself to bring the character of faraway eastern lands home. This simple construction of a Chinese pavilion, and the planting around it, centres the vision of the modern world on what was not so simple a century ago or even in the early years of the 20th century.

Nature writers tend to exclude this cultural dimension and emphasise only the inherent habits of avifauna, fauna and plants. But why not let the imagination go beyond and create presences? The Greeks and Romans of the ancient world peopled the natural with glimpses of gods and goddesses. They liked what is in essence unexplained and caused vegetation to harbour unseen legends. In contrast, a small thing in the garden, a pot of clay, or suchlike, concentrates the mind on materials that do not move or alter. This is very different from being confronted by Apollo or Daphne, their lurking or their vanishing. Yet contrasts in material alone can startle, can bring on new thoughts. A pause does everyone much good. Anyway, nature does well in a pot. It heightens the effect of the plant we put there.

The humble pot is a feature normally used on a smaller scale. It has colour and design. This combination of shiny exterior and the plant chosen to take advantage of it, can bring an intimate touch of humanity among wilder, self-seeding flowers or foliage. Mine are set among blue bugle or yellow comfrey – and there is the occasional nettle, but the butterfly breeds there and this does not come amiss. The best idea is to have several pots grouped together. Then you have an intervention of colour and the blooms you want.

The natural world takes hold in the garden anyway, and today it is appreciated once more. Setting cultivars in pots and having grasses and wildflowers growing around them is often appealing as the green laps up to naturalise the pots. I have some roses in blue, big pots. They grow with wild pansies that have self-seeded and now yellow cowslips have suddenly appeared at the base of the pot.

In a nook and cranny that shuns flowers used to much light, ferns with their unfolding light green croziers in spring might bring a focal point and lead on to a meditation on caring. The staff held aloft was a symbol for shepherds and so also of those, like bishops or carers. Flowers, such as the violet, rose and lily were also. It does them reverence if we treat them as more than themselves and watch them thrive in special pots.

In my East Lothian garden, I have added flying ironwork butterflies to the house to make it less serious. This gives a flutter or a lift to all heavy thoughts. You are linked repeatedly, having this image on the wall, with the idea that in the natural world, too, there are buzzing and flying invertebrates like your thoughts – they may rise in the air where they will. My butterflies are not high art but an intervention that commentates on my plants and garden layout.

Let us concentrate for a moment on pathways in the garden. Little Sparta has brick ways and stones. They lead in different ways to the episodes of carved inscriptions that accompany the garden's varied spaces. They guide our access and determine how to look and how to raise the eye. Then the planting augments the carvings and the rest of the thinking is done in the mind of the visitor. Pathways can be humble or grand. Ian Finlay includes the sight of Scottish lochs in his planting of yellow flag irises, not an uncommon flower in the wet moors of higher land.

Pathways, views, statues, columns and inscriptions add another dimension to a garden beyond the underlying design. I remember seeing an 18th-century rendition of Flora, wedged in between houses built beside what is now the altered approach to a landscape garden in Germany. The statue was situated in a wild part of the garden, no flowerbeds created about her. Nonetheless she enhanced the wildwood to such an extent that even many years later I see her striding the woods and making them come alive. The young trees and shrubland would not have evidenced the same verdant growth, it seemed to me, without her striding in glory through these small woodlands.

The same is true of a statue of the goddess Diana in the same landscape garden. She is there in the landscape as a white presence with her arm out-stretched and a hunting dog looking up at her. She is among the bracken and in front of trees – a hunting scenario. One could imagine wild boar or deer in the distance. Again, the statue lends credence and the validity of the mythic to the idea of chasing wildlife. It would have been an empty stretch at the edge of the woods without her.

To add another plane, objects and sculpture can raise flowers, or shrubs or trees to contemplation. Or the other way around, sculpture or objects deliberately placed within a well planted garden are given space to speak. Many museums now have collections featuring sculptures in parks within their grounds. This, of course, is to highlight their holdings of an artist's creation and sculpture retains the focus. The collections are what the museums wish to have scrutinised or admired in the landscape. But, of course, the landscape and added plants widen the horizon. A contemporary school of landscape artists such as Charles Jencks bring both aspects into harmony; sculpture and landform coalesce, as in the garden of the Scottish National Gallery of Modern Art, situated above the Water of Leith in Edinburgh.

One of the large landscape gardens in Kassel, Germany, Wilhelmshoehe, is full of sculpture, embracing as its visual focus the rise up a high hill towards its crowning sculpture. The planting of sombre evergreens concentrates the mind. It is hard to see beyond them. The statuary makes its point through its natural elevation. It helps immensely – this high hill. It has as the commanding statue, overlooking all, Hercules with his cudgel. He towers over a cascade that includes Tritons blowing their shells with the water plunging downhill, to finally end in a pool where the statue of Neptune reigns. Landscape in this garden is overseen by Hercules, whose labours the local sovereign wished to claim.

Historic gardens, as we have seen, often featured sculpture within parterres or formal planting. The interaction of garden and sculpture are unified and seek to bring out thoughts and feelings through their coordination. The planting is often aligned with the landscape to further the silent message of the sculpture. But there is also sculpture in historic landscape gardens that is not statuary, anticipating Jencks and the modern school. Sculpture can be in the form of cut-out lakes, such as crescent moons. Studley Royal displays moon crescent shapes and a temple as it recedes from the ruin of an abbey. These are not sculptures in the normal sense. Artificial lakes made in accord with the concept of garden designers are artistic symbols which look good and at the same time draw the observer further than the natural forms alone would suggest.

This should be an inspiration. The Royal Botanic Garden

Edinburgh will lead you on pathways in which you can experience the great variety of plants, including those of foreign nations. They have achieved over time the sinuousness of a meander among plants. As you saunter, you find instruction, and never to be forgotten is their origin in the botanic garden of physicians. Now we have the pathways and beds and even glass houses for exotic plants that cannot survive Scottish winters. The garden has become a place of learning and appreciation for public and specialists alike. But there are also sculptures and art objects carefully placed, such as the monument to Linnaeus which commemorates the ordering of science while acknowledging life's passing. Sculpture, in its many forms, is an apt addition to such a natural treasure house and people come to draw and paint and photograph their own creative responses.

I especially like the puzzle and inspiration of sculpture among plants. It embellishes the meaning of growing things to have them transported in the mind through statuary and other designed objects, including even the landform itself. Sculpture creates gestures in the mind without the constraints of language. This form of silent expression in a garden is a kind of freedom and it adds to our knowledge and wellbeing. Gardens are by nature quiet places and it is up to us to explore them and to be inspired by them. I hope these various ways to look at gardens encourages the imagination. Seeing is certainly more than perceiving what is in front of us. Landscapes, buildings and sculptures promote multiple visions. To look closely means to open new windows into the mind and to spark creativity. Art in all its forms illuminates why gardens matter so much to humankind.

Community Gardens
by Donald Smith

IN THIS FINAL CHAPTER, we trace the origins of another contemporary aspect of gardening. It is remarkable that in a new social context and form the all-round importance of gardens quickly re-asserts itself and flourishes.

The communal or collective use of land to grow food has a long pedigree. Peasant economies were based on this practice though often it was subordinate to a set of obligations or payments. In modern industrial economies, usually in urban contexts, the allotments system sought to re-enact some heritage of community use. However, this was also based on land-owning rights retained by municipalities or corporations. In neither case were the users, the front line cultivators, owners. They were granted rights of use by a landlord.

In the 19th and 20th centuries, these powers became increasingly concentrated in fewer hands, public and private. Consequently, a movement towards community ownership began in order to try and redress that balance. Community gardens, in distinction from allotments, may owe their origins to a 1960s upsurge in community-based action, reacting to the increasing role of governments and the rapidly increasing power of multi-national companies. Somewhere between these two forces, the customs or conventions of local influence and control were squeezed out, provoking a more radical renewal of the communal.

Community gardening, therefore, has to be seen alongside community farms, woodlands, housing associations, community arts and education, community health and community development projects in terms of motivation and objectives.

However, community gardening has some distinctive features which also contribute to the evolution of gardens. The community garden movement is forming another chapter in the story of gardens.

From the start the aim was more than food production. But benefits of local growing were related to health and wellbeing. The food produced locally was responsibly sourced, based often on organic horticulture, so maximising nutritional benefit while avoiding the negative side effects of industrialised farming and genetic uniformity.

In addition, the collective activity of growing and harvesting this produce was understood as a contribution to healthy living. This ranges from the physical benefits of exercise, through the psychological benefits of communal activity, to a potential spiritual benefit of living in closer contact with nature as well as one's fellow humans. As we shall see creativity and culture also come into play, because social activity always has a cultural aspect.

It was this spectrum of engagement that inspired the Scottish International Storytelling Festival's 'Healing Gardens' programme in Edinburgh, and it is from this remarkable city that examples are drawn. Joanna Geyer-Kordesch's contribution was to reveal the long layering of this theme, helping the gardeners themselves reflect on the back story of their own contemporary struggles and aspirations.

In focusing on Edinburgh case studies, however, it is important to acknowledge some generally Scottish influences, reaching back through the Industrial Revolution to the 18th century Enlightenment and 16th century Protestant Reformation.

The Reformation in Scotland ushered in a Presbyterian system of church and parish (local neighbourhood) government, that strongly emphasised collective responsibility. The objective was not an isolated godliness but a society at local and national levels devoted to the 'commonweal' or commonwealth. This involved drawing on landed wealth, including land owned by the church, to support education and social welfare. In these aspects at least, the Scottish Reformation did not lead to individualism but to an even stronger version of the social responsibility espoused by medieval Roman Catholic teaching.

While this ethos often sustained a status quo dominated by wealthy, hereditary landowners, it also implied a wider field of obligation. In addition, a tradition of radical dissent was born, including at times collective resistance against unjust authority. When industrialisation disrupted older social patterns, the sense of religious, moral obligation was carried forward by new voluntary movements. They paradoxically challenged the older Presbyterian establishment, while at the same time applying its core values in new urban contexts.

Industrialisation and urbanisation proceeded at an exceptionally rapid pace in Scotland as the nation's abundant natural resources were harnessed to the economic expansion of Britain's burgeoning Empire. The social and human dislocation was all the more abrupt, prompting in turn radical communal movements such as the Chartists, early Trade Unionism, the Co-operative Societies and finally the Independent Labour Party. None of these initiatives were exempt from the deeply moral impulses of Presbyterianism.

Pre-eminent, if not notorious, in this rapid modernisation was the emigration and then clearance of traditional Highland society. This meant peasants and the tacksmen – that is clan land managers – were cleared from their age-old holdings. This proved to be a brutal exercise of power driven by the need for estate owners to put profit before people. The victims were powerless because the clan system had been systematically undermined, while the people of Scotland had no effective political representation apart from the vested interests which were enforcing the clearances.

Eventually a bottom up resistance movement took effect, based on renewing the principal of collective rights through crofting (ie small holding tenure) and in some cases, as at Glendale in Skye, communal ownership of estates. Land agitations led to the 1880s Napier Commission which enshrined crofting tenure in law. This led in time to further legal rights and instruments of collective ownership, which were significantly boosted by the re-instated Scottish Parliament from its inception in 1999. As we shall see these historic factors continue to shape community gardening in Scotland because of the strong link between communal use and community ownership.

One factor in the continuing identity in Scotland between land and people is the lack of any exclusively urban sensibility. Scotland is a nation of mountains, rivers and lochs, and all of its conurbations are within easy reach of natural landscapes, often enjoying dramatic natural settings. Edinburgh, the capital city, is no exception in this regard. Built on a post-volcanic geoscape, it has Arthur's Seat at its centre and is surrounded by hill ranges and an impressive firth or estuary opening to the North Sea. These aspects of the city, and of Scotland's sense of itself, are brilliantly evoked by Enrico Miralles' design for the new Scottish Parliament building that nestles below Arthur's Seat and points out towards the sea. Its grounds merge artfully into the apparently wild landscape of the Royal Park, encompassing also the sea views beloved by Scotland's landscape gardens.

In the medieval period when the burgh of Edinburgh first took root, every dwelling had a landholding or 'tenement' behind it. Even as population density increased, gardens remained a critical part of the early modern townscape, so that when, in the 18th century, the classical ideal of *rus in urbe* (country in the city) took hold, Edinburgh was well positioned to oblige. Because of its setting, Edinburgh's 19th century expansion absorbed a number of landscaped estates into its boundaries providing many green areas. In the late 19th and early 20th centuries, the pioneer sociologist and town planner, Patrick Geddes, campaigned to create communal gardens space – 'green lungs' – in the poorest and most overcrowded parts of the city centre.

Consequently, when we consider community gardens in Edinburgh today, we can see that they are part of the city's character, while also belonging firmly in the wider European narrative. It is also interesting that the land available in the early modern period in Edinburgh for collective use derived from either church or monarchy. Some of the urban holdings of the monasteries and friaries passed into ownership of the Town Council, while the transfer of the Scottish monarchs to London made the extensive gardens at Holyroodhouse Palace redundant as a royal pleasure ground. As previously noted, the first Botanic Garden in Edinburgh used the grounds of Trinity College Church in the valley between Calton Hill and the Royal Mile, as well as the redundant gardens around Holyroodhouse. The gardens on which Mary Queen of Scots once lavished so much attention and care in memory of her gardening mother, now accommodate the modern Scottish Parliament.

To illustrate contemporary garden developments, I shall look at four Edinburgh examples. They are Dr Neil's Garden in Duddingston, the Lochend Secret Garden, Leith Community Crops in Pots and the Royal Botanic Garden's Community Garden.

Dr Neil's Garden was the initiative of a husband and wife team of general practitioners, Doctors Nancy and Andrew Neil. Their medical practice was in Meadowbank, a densely populated urban area on the north side of Arthur's Seat. They were both enthusiastic leisure gardeners and travellers, who collected plants and young trees on European holidays. In 1963, while still fully engaged with medical work, they also began work in a field on the south side of Arthur's Seat, immediately above Duddingston Loch. This land was part of the glebe (church land) of the medieval parish church of Duddingston, once a village on the outskirts of Edinburgh. The ground, known as The Calves Field, is steep and rocky and had only ever been used for grazing. Despite this it was a striking location stretching down from where Duddingston

Kirk still stands on its rocky knoll, to the main natural water feature of the Royal Park.

Over a long period, the venture attracted more volunteers and an astonishing transformation unfolded with the planting of trees and shrubs, in an evolving design that gradually turned the barren rocky slopes into a series of winding paths, groves and terraced features. Within the pattern a vegetable and herb area emerged with cold frames and the capacity to generate new plants from seed. Nonetheless, Dr Neil's Garden is above all a landscape garden, inspired by its location and the Romantic tradition. This is now strongly articulated by the natural look of the mature trees. In reality the Royal Park area had been denuded of natural tree cover for centuries.

For Doctors Neil the health benefits of gardening were clearly in mind for themselves and others, but equally, if not more importantly, was enjoying, and creating natural beauty. The support of the Church was important and an open, ecumenical spirituality was implied but never imposed. These combined purposes led in due course to the formation of a charity to sustain what is now an outstanding feature of Edinburgh's landscape.

The influence of Dr Neil's Garden subsequently spread to the rest of the Duddingston glebe land with the enthusiastic encouragement of the parish minister Dr James Jack, who is also an architect. The Manse Garden adjacent to Dr Neil's provided a complement and access to the landscape garden, while the other glebe fields are now home to a young orchard and a community vegetable garden. There is an ambition to find appropriate landscape garden forms that express the social and spiritual aspects of these more recent developments which are being directly undertaken by the Church.

In retrospect Dr Neil's Garden is one of the earliest examples in Scotland of what was to develop as a contemporary community garden. However, its origins lie in personal initiative and philanthropy, linking to the traditional communal ownership inherited by the Church. In the Scottish social context, it began as an essentially middle-class venture, underpinned by leisure and charity.

A very contrasting picture emerges if we return back across Arthur's Seat to Lochend, a locality adjacent to Meadowbank in the direction of Leith, the port of Edinburgh on the Firth of Forth. Lochend was originally a castled estate that passed into the ownership of Edinburgh City Council in the 1920s. The land was used to build local authority owned housing, replacing the tenement flats in older overcrowded areas of the city. The layout of the new housing estate was generous in terms of open space, parks and gardens. These echoed the shared back greens of the older tenement flats, while aspiring towards rural greening in the 'garden city' mode, of which there are comparable examples in Rosyth in Fife and Pollok in Glasgow.

From the 1980s when the UK Government introduced a tenants' Right to Buy scheme, many houses passed into private ownership and the traditional communality of housing estates like these waned. This left common areas underused or neglected, and in due course this created opportunities for a contemporary community garden. In the early 21st century however, the climate of public policy and funding had radically changed since the Doctors Neil initiated their Duddingston Garden.

The Lochend community gardeners were supported from 2011 by the Central Scotland Green Network (CSGN), an umbrella for community gardens and woodlands, renewable energy and other environmental projects across the post-industrial landscape of the Central Lowlands. CSGN is actively encouraged as an instrument of the Scottish Government's policies and was able to secure grant aid for Lochend's new 'Secret Garden'. The secret refers to the garden's location in the centre of the estate tucked behind the houses in what is called the Quadrant.

The Lochend Community Garden has an array of more than 50 raised beds looked after by individuals, families, informal groups or other community organisations, numbering over 100 people in total. The ethos is of growth, balance, wellbeing and relaxation with individuals being encouraged to participate for reasons of physical and mental health. Vegetables, herbs and flowers all feature. The environmental benefits are also foregrounded, and at the start of 2017 further public grant support was secured, channelled towards 'community growing'. This gives the venture at least another five years of growing space.

Obtaining time limited project grants is very challenging for community projects that lack other financial resources. So the lobbying and policy development role of networks like CSGN is vital in enabling support from different kinds of funds, re-pre-senting or re-focusing core purposes. The inherent strength or ap-peal of such ventures lies in their large volunteer base and broad social impacts, but without the public policy climate created by the Scottish Parliament and Government, and the active partici-pation of other social funders, many of these community gardens might not survive.

Continuing northwards from Lochend we reach Leith and another, much more visible, community garden sited at the west-ern edge of Leith Links. This large area of public parkland is not only Council-owned but held under strict longstanding legal conditions known in Scotland as 'Common Good'. The two acres now cultivated by Leith Community Crops in Pots contained ten-nis courts and other sporting facilities which were moved, leaving the ground disused and covered with hard surfaces.

The challenging opportunity offered by a derelict area of over two acres was taken up by a small community group that had begun some two years earlier in another part of Leith. On Junction Street, in the centre of Leith's traditional working-class community, there were two adjacent courtyards, which had once formed part of Dr Bell's School, the gift of a Victorian philan-thropist Andrew Bell who pioneered educational provision for India's urban poor. Passing eventually into local authority owner-ship, one courtyard was attached to flats owned by Port of Leith Housing Association and one to Stanwell Nursery School.

A single parent, Evie Murray, who was caring for her own and a friend's children, began to turn the flats' courtyard into garden space for growing low cost nutritious food. Other par-ents became involved and the Headteacher of the nursery, Alison Smith, opened up the adjacent courtyard for the same purpose, attracting in the process a much wider network of interest and support. From these small, practical beginnings Leith Communi-ty Crops in Pots was formed as a charity in 2013.

The gardening activities spread to other local schools with

the emphasis placed on healthy activity and nutrition, based primarily on raised beds. However, the Leith Links site was of a different scale and required a huge initial effort. Apart from the extensive area of gravel the soil was sandy and covered with a stubborn well-established layer of turf and thistles. Work began in 2013, and with over 100 committed volunteers, the transformation was remarkable, creating productive vegetable-growing plots and flowering banks formed from the turf cover. Social and play areas followed along with an orchard and soft fruit area. Practical problems included an inadequate water supply and a crumbling sports pavilion still in intermittent use for junior football. Ambitions for a market garden and café are active but still unfulfilled at the time of writing.

The work with local schools also continued through this period and none of the changes could have been achieved without significant support from the Scottish Government's Climate Challenge Fund, several charitable trusts and some social enterprise investment. Equally Leith Community Crops in Pots is wholly dependent on its volunteers and 'urban crofters'. That description is significant as the organisation prides itself on its radical activism in the tradition of the Highland crofters. Democratic decision-making is sometimes difficult to reconcile with the governance requirements of a constituted charity, but it is interesting to note that Evie Murray remains a moving force in the organisation and that other founding supporters are still committed and involved. The people factor remains essential in making the systems work. The results, however, are evident for all to see, in terms of productivity and colourful greening in place of disuse and dereliction. Perhaps one of the main impacts of this community garden is its visibility and physical openness to a wide cross-section of local society.

Visibility and public openness is central to the fourth Edinburgh example, the Royal Botanic Garden Edinburgh (RBGE), situated now at Inverleith, west of Leith Links and the mouth of the Water of Leith. The origins of the garden in botany and medicine are part of the European narrative already related, but in the new millennium RBGE has also become an active community garden. Activities, including school and volunteer plots, and horticultural education, are grouped in a distinct area behind the garden's famous beech hedge. In addition, as of 2016, the centrepiece of this area has become the restored Botanic Cottage, which was rescued from dereliction at the previous location of Edinburgh's Botanic Garden, established by John Hope, on Leith Walk. The restored cottage provides a superb community facility, and potentially a networking focus for community gardeners, as during the Scottish International Storytelling Festival.

However, the input of Jenny Foulkes, the Community Gardening support worker at RBGE, at these events, was not about the dissemination of horticultural expertise. Rather her emphasis was on giving people an experience of the natural world, a sense of connection and value. The physical sensations of gardening – hands in the soil – were cited as restorative. Combined with the communality of working together and the 'something additional' – the 'magic' of helping things grow – the total experience led to discernible improvements in physical and mental health.

Jane Mather, a mental health support worker, articulated the same experiences in relation to the Lochend Secret Garden. Although horticultural practice and healthy eating were integral to the project aims, it was the sense of 'connection with natural cycles' that added 'the magic ingredient', 'the stress buster.' The garden had also become a focus for creative play, a safe space in contact with natural energies and beauty. While Evie Murray's account of Leith Community Crops in Pots stressed issues of land ownership, environmental sustainability and social equity, she also spoke about a 'nature deficit disorder' and the psychological healing involved in restoring a direct experience of the natural world and its growth cycles.

It was plain that the impulse towards healing experiences was central to the community garden initiatives. Such testimonies led naturally to discussion of the contemporary relevance of community gardens to medical care. Again, Edinburgh has an interesting example in the Redhall Walled Garden on the south side of the city which is run by the Scottish Association for Mental Health and contributes to the therapeutic treatment of those with long-term recovery challenges.

Medical professionals at every level seem more open to the role of such therapies and potentially to the prescription of gardening or creative activities alongside, or in place of, more conventional treatments. Many hospitals and health boards are also landowners with the capacity to use their own grounds more creatively and productively.

While welcoming all these possibilities, the community gardeners were also keen to emphasise the broad inclusivity of their spaces. For some the benefit of participation is the benefit of working or socialising with others who are not in their existing contact groups, situation or perhaps mindset. This applies to age, gender, physical capability, ethnicity, health and socio-economic status. A relaxed exchange of experience can happen within the common space and activity. This broad inclusivity can be a problem in securing some kinds of funding support, since grant-giving bodies often stress in their criteria the need to benefit and so 'target' very specific categories of people. How can that work if collective openness and exchange is the essence?

The openness of the community garden experience – physically, socially and culturally – also invites creative responses. The connection between gardens and art is central to Joanna's thinking, and to her practice as reflected in this book's illustrations. Gardens are a sensory creation appealing to sight, touch, smell and the kinetic awareness of moving round through and within. All of the community gardens discussed generate cultural creativity alongside their other benefits. What is important though is that such activity is not managed or unduly restricted but guided by the initiatives of a wide variety of groups and individuals. Community gardens can become open and shared creative platforms.

The Royal Botanic Garden Edinburgh is home to a number of artistic commissions and exhibitions. For many years its classical villa, once the centre of the Inverleith estate, has been used as an art gallery. But the whole garden is a hive of art classes, poetry, storytelling and quiet reflection. The education and events programme partners with many cultural organisations, while the community garden space with its Botanic Cottage allows this to happen in many informal ways. Each year the Scottish International Storytelling Festival responds to some thematic aspect of RBGE's identity, history or design, while regularly co-hosting with the Garden's public events programme a day of family activity. This offers storytelling and musical experiences appropriate to the diverse neuks, glades and landscape features, all encountered in a relaxed 'happening upon' style that evokes spirit of place.

Equally, Dr Neil's Garden is home to many creative groups and activities. Especially notable on the wider Duddingston site is a long association with Theatre Alba. This pioneering theatre company, founded in 1981 by the late Charles Nowosielski, has been producing site-specific drama at Duddingston since 1998. This includes promenade performances in Dr Neil's Garden evoking the sense of magic which gardens provide in children's literature, and full scale plays superbly adapted for performance in the Manse Garden and lochside spaces. Theatre Alba combines drama professionals with community actors and a huge network of volunteers from Church and community who enable this festival of garden theatre to take place in a way that both respects and enhances the site.

At Lochend Secret Garden, Jane Mather has played a key role in fostering creative activity for families. Combining her skills as a support worker and oral storyteller, she has focused on the same 'sense of magic' experienced in the natural world to nurture imagination and its expressions. Her storytelling approach is not to impose a particular narrative but to let the stories arise from responses to the garden. Lochend as a location does not have the same prominence as some of the other Edinburgh gardens, and consequently attracts fewer established arts groups. Nonetheless, Jane cites the way in which the children themselves are now drawn to the garden as a place of free creative play. This link between the layout of community gardens, play and creativity is a common thread, though staunch community horticulturalists sometimes need to be won over to the vital importance of providing spaces within the garden for free play.

The large two-acre site of Leith Community Crops in Pots offers plenty of unstructured play opportunities, as well as the visual stimuli of a design still in the making. The organisation embraces artwork as a means of conveying the lively mix of flower, fruit and vegetables across the site through drawing and photography. These give the website a distinctive character.

There are regular family events on 'the Croft' involving craft, storytelling and music. In the ethos of 'urban crofters' the Leith garden draws on customs from Scotland's traditional seasonal festivals such as Beltane/Mayday and Samhainn/Hallowe'en. These happenings are part of a wider cultural movement to re-establish patterns of environmental connection. This may involve sourcing and re-introducing in new ways discontinued customs such as wassailing fruit trees in January, or guising at Hallowe'en, which was originally the Celtic New Year.

In summary, it is clear that community gardens reach towards creativity and culture to reflect back and celebrate the range of ways in which they contribute to wellbeing. The environmental, nutritional and wider health benefits are not separated out but held holistically within integrating experiences. It is in that process of integration, or re-integration that the healing potential lies. The evidence from all of the Edinburgh case studies points to the centrality of this purpose in the minds and feelings of leaders and participants alike. It is an experience of healing in all its mental, physical, spiritual and social aspects that gives contemporary community gardening hand, heart and soul.

As this book was being edited for publication the coronavirus Covid 19 came to Britain with devastating impacts on physical and mental health. The accompanying lockdown severely restricted economic and social activities. Some community gardens have had to close completely, but those that belong to community organisations, largely run by volunteer networks, have been able to continue with safe activities. Local garden projects such as Leith Community Crops and Pots have been able to use their knowledge to identify and meet pressing community needs with food deliveries and friendly personal contacts.

As society gradually emerges from the worst stages of this viral crisis, the approaches offered by community gardens to health, wellbeing and environmental sustainability will surely spread. This book has offered many angles, past and present, on why gardens matter, but in the future they are going to matter more than ever.

Epilogue

GARDENS AND THEIR plants enliven us. Their green spaces lure us. And their creativity can lead to our creativity.

They show us not only the peace and quiet that parks or back gardens provide, but also how to focus on slower time – or time in different forms. Now, I am looking back to a time when I was not disabled and then the years when it was very hard to reconcile my body with its restrictions; this last episode was frustrating.

Gardens and plants helped me to redefine how to create new activity and new visions. I'm not claiming it was an easy way forward. But one crucial aspect was to reach beyond being inactive: to see and be part of Nature. To expand my knowledge.

What really helped was to appreciate the growth and the regeneration in winter which spurs new growth in the next spring. This cyclical renewal of plant life tells not only the disabled that it is vital to consciously see the importance of fallow periods and renewed variants of growth. Steps forward need pauses. This is as true of a child learning to walk as it is of a young person choosing their occupation.

I am surrounded by bare-branched trees in the winter. All they do for a time is shake in the wind. If the gusts are strong, they keel far into the heaving wind that roughly combs the twigs and moves stems. In this the trees also clutch the ground. But looking closer at the tops of these trees, you see growing buds that will emerge as green leaves. They are leathery, protecting themselves and growing.

In a period not defined by the clock, but by clouds and sunlight, trees enable themselves to wear their glorious, dishevelled locks and the buds that herald a new season. No haircut needed.

And in autumn leading to winter they drift in bronze, gold, yellow, crazy red singularity and brown despair, dropping and wafting to the ground. Follow that and you are fascinated.

This will draw out some not to be neglected traits. First is observation. Secondly there is the beauty of colours which fascinate and can teach the variants of tints and hues and combinations that are striking. Then all trees learn to withstand tough opposition and so can you. Plants and branches sway in the wind – but their roots clutch fast to an ever-fertile ground.

I have come to love what is mute companionship. You learn the language of plants. Their leaves speak to you about how you water, how you mulch, how you prune. The reward is blossom in varied colour and shape. Each plant exhibits its own morphology.

And then you can translate into pencil smudges and drippings of paint the view of each blossom or leaf you choose for illustration. Yes, these happenstances might begin your adventure into creative work – or even become explicit, admirable, drawings and botanical watercolours. But who cares what shape your reaction on paper is?

The courage is to begin and to establish your own handprint and the respect you develop for each plant is your individuality. Creativity is not judged. It is your own doing. What you do – disabled or not – devolves into skill. What you look at closely is inevitably learned by your hand.

❧ ❧ ❧

As with gardens or green spaces, we too are immersed in the hope of season's changing. Even if buried in snow, the landscape is attuned. And we are in it. The black limbs of bare trees wave to us. The wind blows through them, whispering 'Don't forget your wanderings, physically and spiritually. They are never ending.'

And it does not have to be outside. Inside is even richer and more important. That is why everyone should go into a garden or park and look. And I do not preclude that window. It is a framework for your imagination.

I go back in history. It helps to know we have engaged with gardens for centuries. They provide an indisputable characteristic: looking at what you see. Landscape gardens in particular show how much thought it took to group characteristics. They help specialise what you encounter or search to find – or say in your own picture. This can be a note to yourself or a honing of skills on the paper before you.

Yes, I am frustrated that I cannot walk unaided now and sometimes I am not taken seriously just because I am in a wheelchair. It is horrible that physical disablement reigns over mental capacity when the outside world looks at you. But there are ways around things that can be invented. And circumvention can be creative. I have experienced kindness and attention at garden centres when I say that botanical nomenclature is confusing and

nothing like seeing the plant itself. And I am given a lot of help when I go wheeling up to a pot and choosing it!

Disability is limiting, but despite this, people are willing to talk with you and you with them. All of a sudden and with little introduction.

Plants are a good third party. Silent in staring at you, upwardly mobile as you immerse them in garden soil. They are as talkative as you are, but let you decide how to admire them. Their language is blooms and leaves. Yours is to chatter – either to them, about them, or in the air talking poetry since it's the best way to describe them. They will allow you peace and your own creativity.

Being a couch potato is no way to engage or perceive, make yourself heard, or enjoy the very new colours of a very new plant that has just been pointed out to you. Make way to the green space that enriches what you are.

❧ ❧ ❧

I walked landscape gardens for many years seeing how various designed landscapes affected me. I went to Painshill, Rousham, Stowe, Stourhead, Studley Royal, Inverary, Dunkeld, Culzean Castle, Dessau-Woerlitz and Sansouci in Germany and landscape gardens in Austria and more. This was before I had my stroke. Then I read about landscape gardens like Versailles near Paris and Little Sparta in Scotland. Disability and a wheelchair do restrict you in walking any paths not level or smoothed out. But not all is inaccessible.

If nothing else, you can enjoy the more prominent landscape gardens through pictures and photographs in the many books produced. Old and new ones show them in their seasons and often accentuate their temples and sightlines, statues, lakes and strategically placed trees. There is no harm in piling up these nice books and enjoying a landscape garden this way – and you might be the perfect person to tell another why these places intrigued you so much.

I wrote this book because I wanted to engage others with the joys of looking around green spaces. Painting and talking about plants makes me happy, and allows me to explore the spaces close to me, along with the many meaningful vistas that are incorporated into grand landscape gardens. They disclose more and more meanings as you get to know them. And the peace and imaginative stimulation of all plant-rich places have lasted for so many centuries. Then and now. Enjoy!

POEMS

May

Cold or not, May
Seethes in greenery
Winds noticeably combing
Lawns and new leaves

Can't save yourself from thistles or violets,
Indiscriminate lot, growing everywhere
Drinking rain, spurting up, breathing green,
Hope eternal,
Seeds everywhere.

Weeping Copper Beech

Dark hanging leaves
Deep and veined oracles
Travelling downwards towards the earth
Branches drooping, negating
Uplift, scrolling messages
Bronze definitions
Of what the beech should be:
Story lines in leaf
In straight rills
Fanning outwards.

Trees

Light green in the beeches
Leaves unfurling
So definite, so slow, so stealthy but
Spring overpowering me.

I look and look
And see light in buds held high
Then those sharpened quills

The writing of trees
Unsheathing in uncurling leaves,
The writing in the wind,

Written words in woodland,
Swirling, whirling me away,
The voluptuous multitude,
Viridian and beyond it cerulean,
The blue sky endless.

❦

Sources and Further Reading

Note: This book is for the general reader and for those interested in gardens. It is based on many of the following books but I did not want it overloaded with footnotes.

Arber, AR, 'Herbals: Their Origin and Evolution' in *The History of Botany, 1470–1670*, first published 1912, reprint Cambridge, 2012.

Arnold, D (ed.), *The Georgian Villa*, Gloucestershire, 1996.

Baker, S, *The Country Houses, Castles and Mansions of East Lothian*, Stenlake, 2009.

Bannerman, J, *The Beatons: A Medical Kindred in the Classical Gaelic Tradition*, 2015.

BB (Denys Watkins-Pitchford), *The Little Grey Men*, first published 1942, new edition Oxford, 2012.

Beith, M, *Healing Threads: Traditional Medicines of the Highlands and Islands*, Edinburgh, 1995.

Bennett, J, *The Writer's Garden: How Gardens Inspired our Best-Loved Authors*, London, 2014.

van Berkel, K, and Vanderjagt, A (eds), *The Book of Nature in Early Modern and Modern History*, Paris, 2006.

Blunt, W, and Stearn, WT, *The Art of Botanical Illustration*, London, new and revised edition 1994.

Boney, AD, *The Lost Gardens of Glasgow University*, London, 1988.

Boston, LM, *Memories: Incorporating Perverse and Foolish and Memory in a House*, Cambridge, 1992.

Boston, LM, *The Children of Green Knowe and The River at Green Knowe*, first published 1954 and 1959 respectively, now republished together London, 2015.

Bowden, JK, and Lightfoot, J, *His Work and Travels, with a Biographical Introduction and a Catalogue of the Lightfoot Herbarium*, Kew, 1989.

de Bray, L, *The Art of Botanical Illustration: A History of the Classical Illustrators and their Achievements*, new edition, London, 2005.

Brown, J, *The Pursuit of Paradise: A Social History of Gardens and Gardening*, London, 1999.

Brown, M, *Scotland's Lost Gardens: From the Garden of Eden to the Stewart Palaces*, Edinburgh, 2012.

Campbell, G, *The Hermit in the Garden: From Imperial Rome to Ornamental Gnome*, Oxford, 2013.

Chambers, D, *The Planters of the English Landscape Garden, Botany, Trees, and the Georgics*, London, 1993.

Clark, K, *Landscape into Art*, London, 2013.

Cosgrove, D, and Daniels, S (eds.), *The Iconography of Landscape*, Cambridge, 1988.

Coventry, M, *The Castles of Scotland: A Comprehensive Guide to more than 4,100 Castles, Towers, Historic Houses, Stately Homes and Family Lands*, first published 1995, 5th edition Prestonpans, 2015.

Delumeaun, J, *History of Paradise: The Garden of Eden in Myth and Tradition*, translated from the French by Matthew O'Connell, Chicago, IL, 2000.

Dendle, R, and Touwaide, A (eds.), *Health and Healing from the Medieval Garden*, Woodbridge, Suffolk, 2008.

Desmond, R, *Great Natural History Books and their Creators*, London, 2003.

Desmond, R, *The History of the Botanic Gardens Kew*, London, 1995, paperback edition 1998.

Dixon Hunt, J, *Gardens and the Picturesque, Studies in the History of Landscape Architecture*, Cambridge, MA, 2nd printing, 1997.

Dixon Hunt, J, *The Figure in the Landscape, Poetry, Painting,* and *Gardening During the Eighteenth Century*, Baltimore, MD, first published 1976, paperback 1989.

Douglas Wiggin, K, *Rebecca of Sunnybrook Farm*, first published 1923, new edition London, 2014.

Enge, TO, and Schroeder, CF, *Garden Architecture in Europe 1450–1800, From the Villa Garden of the Italian Renaissance to the English Landscape Garden*, London, 1992.

Fairchild Ruggles, D, *Islamic Gardens and Landscapes*, Philadelphia, PA, 2008.

Haldane, E, *Scots Gardens in Old Times (1200–1800)*, London, 1934.

Harper, F, (ed.), *The Travels of William Bartram* (shortened title), 1998.

Harris, E, *The Country Houses of Robert Adam*, London, 2007.

Harris, J, and Snodin, M (eds), *Sir William Chambers, Architect to George III*, London, 1996.

Harvey, J, *Medieval Gardens*, London, 1981.

Hatfield, M, *Landscape with Trees*, London, 1967.

Haydon, R, *Mrs Delany and Her Flower Collages*, first published 1980, new edition London, 1992.

Hewlings, R, *Chiswick House and Gardens*, London, 1989.

Hibbert, C, *Versailles*, New York, 1972.

Hodgson Burnett, F, *The Secret Garden*, London, n.d., illustrated by Inga Moore.

Holland Braund, KE, and Porter, CM (eds.), *Fields of Vision: Essays on the Travels of William Bartram*, Tuscaloosa, AL, 2010.

Jennings, A, *Medieval Gardens*, London, 2004.

Judd, D and Uttley, A, *Spinner of Tales: The Authorized Biography of the Creator of Little Grey Rabbit*, first published 1986, new edition Manchester, 2010.

Kern, H, *Through the Labyrinth: Designs and Meanings Through 5,000 Years*, English edition London, 2000.

Lablaude, P-A, *The Gardens of Versailles*, first published 1995, new edition Paris, 2005.

Laird, M, and Weisberg-Roberts, A (eds.), *Mrs. Delany and Her Circle*, London, 2010.

Landsberg, S, *The Medieval Garden*, London, n. d.

Lindsay, I, and Cosh, M, *Inverary and the Dukes of Argyll*, Edinburgh, 1973.

Masset, C, *Orchards*, Oxford, 2012.

McBride, D, *What They Did with Plants, A Link with Ireland's Past*, Banbridge, 1991.

Mowl, T, *Gentlemen Gardeners: The Men Who Created the English Landscape Garden*, first published 2000, republished Gloucestershire 2010.

Musgrave, T, *Paradise Gardens, Spiritual Inspiration and Earthly Expression*, London, 2015.

Musgrave, T, and Gardner, C, *The Plant Hunters: Two Hundred Years of Adventure and Discovery around the World*, London, 1998.

Noltie HJ and Morton, AG, *Memoir of a Scottish Botanist: John Hope (1725–1786)*, new and revised edition Edinburgh, 2011.

Omand, D (ed.) *The Argyll Book*, Edinburgh, 2004.

Pearce, D, *The Great Houses of London*, first published 1986, paperback New York, 2001.

Pearce, P, *Tom's Midnight Garden*, first published 1958, new edition Oxford, 2008.

Prest, J, *The Garden of Eden: The Botanic Garden and the Recreation of Paradise*, London, 1981.

Quin, T, *BB Remembered: The Life and Times of Denys Watkins-Pitchford*, Shrewsbury, 2006.

Robertson, FW, *Early Scottish Gardeners and their Plants 1650–1750*, East Lothian, 2000.

Royal Botanic Garden Edinburgh, *The Book of the Scottish Garden*, first published 1989, republished Edinburgh, 1997.

Sanders, R, *Flowers: A Celebration of Botanical Art*, English edition, translated by Peter Lewis, text by Andreas Honegger, London, 2016.

Sanderson, MHB, *Robert Adam and Scotland: Portrait of an Architect*, first published 1992, reprint Edinburgh, 1993.

Sheeler, J, *Little Sparta: A Guide to the Garden of Ian Hamilton Finlay*, Edinburgh, 2015.

Sheeler, J, *Little Sparta: The Garden of Ian Hamilton Finlay*, London, 2003.

Sherwood, S, *Contemporary Botanical Artists*, London, 1996.

Symes, M, *The Picturesque and the Later Georgian Garden*, Bristol, 2012.

Symes, M, and Haines, S, *Enville, Hagley, The Leasowes: Three Eighteenth Century Gardens*, Bristol, 2010.

Tait, AA, *The Landscape Garden in Scotland, 1735–1835*, Edinburgh, 1980.

The National Trust, *Stowe Landscape Gardens*, Stowe, n.d.

Way, T, *The Tudor Garden, 1485–1603*, Oxford, 2013.

West, K, *How to Draw Plants: The Techniques of Botanical Illustration*, London, 1983.

Woodbridge, K, *Landscape and Antiquity, Aspects of English Culture at Stourhead 1718–1838*, Oxford, 1970.

☙

Luath Press Limited

committed to publishing well written books worth reading

LUATH PRESS takes its name from Robert Burns, whose little collie Luath (*Gael.*, swift or nimble) tripped up Jean Armour at a wedding and gave him the chance to speak to the woman who was to be his wife and the abiding love of his life. Burns called one of the 'Twa Dogs' Luath after Cuchullin's hunting dog in Ossian's *Fingal*. Luath Press was established in 1981 in the heart of Burns country, and is now based a few steps up the road from Burns' first lodgings on Edinburgh's Royal Mile. Luath offers you distinctive writing with a hint of unexpected pleasures.

Most bookshops in the UK, the US, Canada, Australia, New Zealand and parts of Europe, either carry our books in stock or can order them for you. To order direct from us, please send a £sterling cheque, postal order, international money order or your credit card details (number, address of cardholder and expiry date) to us at the address below. Please add post and packing as follows: UK – £1.00 per delivery address; overseas surface mail – £2.50 per delivery address; overseas airmail – £3.50 for the first book to each delivery address, plus £1.00 for each additional book by airmail to the same address. If your order is a gift, we will happily enclose your card or message at no extra charge.

Luath Press Limited
543/2 Castlehill
The Royal Mile
Edinburgh EH1 2ND
Scotland
Telephone: +44 (0)131 225 4326 (24 hours)
Email: sales@luath. co.uk
Website: www.luath.co.uk